CRYING ...
HOW TO COPE

Pat Gray has had two crying babies and for the past five years has helped run CRY-SIS, the national support group for parents of crying babies.

She knows how it feels to have a crying baby, what the problems are and what the long-term effects can be. In her easy-to-read book, written to help parents as well as their babies, she explains why babies cry and what can be done to help.

Before having her family, Pat Gray worked for eight years in personnel management and is an Associate Member of the Institute of Personnel Management.

WISEBUY PUBLICATIONS

CRYING BABY
HOW TO COPE

What did we do wrong
To produce such a miserable creature?
What do these Screams mean?
Is this what parenthood is really like?
The pacing the floor
The Screams
The exhaustion
The Screams
The constant feeding
The Screams
The rocking
The Screams
The dummy
The Screams
Why are other mothers so organised,
So clean and tidy,
So glamorous.
Oh my aching back,
My knotted stomach.
My tears
My baby's tears
Never ending tears
Why does no one understand?
"Well all babies cry sometime"
"You just have to be firm"
They just have no conception of what its like.
Well I promise – I do.

Lyn Stacey

CRYING BABY
HOW TO COPE

Pat Gray

WISEBUY PUBLICATIONS

First published 1987

**Further copies of CRYING BABY HOW TO COPE
can be obtained from Wisebuy Publications,
PO Box 379, London NW3 1NJ price £3.50
plus 40p p&p (UK) or £5 (US$8) airmail.**

British Library Cataloguing in Publication Data
Gray, Pat
   Crying Baby How to Cope
   1. Infants – Care and hygiene. 2. Child
   psychology
   I. Title.
   649'. 122'019 RJ61.

   ISBN 0-9509751-3-3

*Typesetting by MC Typeset Ltd, Chatham, Kent.
Printed in Great Britain by Cox & Wyman,
Reading*

Contents

Foreword

Four years ago Rob Buckman interviewed three mothers on Yorkshire TV's 'Where There's Life' about coping with crying babies. As a result the mums formed a local support group which rapidly grew into a national one with hundreds of contacts, local groups and a separate branch in Scotland.

Not content with this impressive record Pat Gray, one of the original three-some and now the group's publicity officer, decided to put down her own experiences and those of others in a book. Here it is.

All babies cry some time, but there is a special breed of wakeful, crying baby. I myself have had two. In the end it's all worth it because these children are usually bright, affectionate and intensely interesting. Now that mine are 14 and 12 and really super people I'm being rewarded for those sleepless nights, but of course you aren't to know that at the time.

How I wish I'd had this book then. It's full of basic common sense advice, useful tricks to try and will be a boon to any mother whether her baby is a 'crier' or not. It's also a very modern book and doesn't fall into the trap of making the baby the centre of attention. Mums, Dads and siblings and families have to cope with a crying baby. The most healthy approach is to teach the baby to fit in as much as possible and become a family member.

One of the most admirable achievements of this helpful book is that it guides you towards that end.

Dr Miriam Stoppard
Presenter of Yorkshire TV's
'Baby & Co' and 'Where There's Life'

Acknowledgements

My grateful thanks go to all the parents who contributed to this book, as well as colleagues in CRY-SIS and many other friends and family who have helped and encouraged me.

I would like especially to thank the doctors, psychologists and health visitors who advised me and read through the draft of this book. My thanks also go to the many organisations and individuals who provided information and to those who checked through relevant sections.

I would like to remember my friend, Alison Liebeskind, who set up CRY-SIS and tragically died two years later. Her kindness and determination has been a great inspiration to me.

Finally, I would like to say a special thank you to my husband, John (who has waited patiently for many a dinner) and to my two lovely ex-criers, Michelle and Daniel.

1

Crying Babies

All babies cry. Some cry more than others. This book is about the ones who cry more. Out of a family of three or four children, often one child appears more difficult and demanding than the others. The baby may cry a great deal or hardly sleep. It may be the first child or the second or even the third or fourth. Parents with other children wonder why this child is so difficult and different from brothers and sisters.

For first-time parents it is even worse. There is nothing to compare the yelling baby with. They blame themselves and their inexperience. Other people may also blame the parents. So the build-up of confidence that is so precious in parenthood is destroyed.

Some babies need more attention than others. Every individual is different. This is not the fault of the baby but a need from within which demands to be fulfilled. Neither is it a fault of the parents who nearly always try their best to meet the needs of their new and much loved infant.

It may seem strange that an entire book can be devoted to this everyday subject – babies' crying. But it is a very big problem, and possibly one of the hardest parents have to face.

Excessive crying is not rare in our society. One in ten babies cry a great deal (much more than is normal) and often for no apparent reason. This leaves many questions unanswered for parents who find that a minor problem for one family has turned into a major catastrophe for them. Are they doing something wrong? Why does *their* baby cry so much? General advice about crying seems inadequate and they are left wondering how to cope with the baby, their feelings and anxieties, as well as the problems that develop with having a crying baby in the house.

The first six months

Although this book is about young babies why cry (that means babies up to six months old) the advice and tips given in the book can be of value to older babies and toddlers as well. The principles are the same – coping with the baby or child and creating a more tolerable existence for yourself.

The first six months of a baby's life are often the most difficult for the parents, with or without an excessively crying baby. After this age, most babies improve (although not all) with physical developments like sitting, crawling and walking. They become more sociable and rewarding between six months and one year. They may still be difficult but there is usually more positive feedback for the parents. If your older baby is still very unhappy and crying a great deal and you feel there has been little or no improvement since the early months, consult your doctor.

Do not believe the 'kind soul' whose words of comfort are 'It only gets worse. You wait until the baby gets older.' These people have not had a crying baby themselves; otherwise they would be more sympathetic. Yes, there are problems with every age, but for many parents the stress and exhaustion of those early months caring for a helpless and demanding baby, who they dearly love, are one of the worst experiences of their lives.

How big is the problem?

Most researchers who study infant behaviour agree that about 10% of babies have what they call 'difficult temperaments' – difficult because they are difficult to care for and to pacify. Within that 10% there are vast differences in behaviour ranging from the colicky baby who cries heartily during one specific time of the day – usually the evening – to the babies who seem to cry every waking moment and to sleep very little indeed.

The other 90% of babies are not of course quiet and magnificently behaved all the time, but they cry much less. Some sleep a great deal between feeds and hardly ever cry; some cry when hungry or tired but seem reasonably content otherwise; some are very wakeful but will lie for hours in your arms or in their prams, looking around at the world or studying their hands or objects close by.

In March 1985 a survey on crying babies published in *Parents Magazine*[1] showed that a staggering 92% of the mothers spent up to 12 hours of every day on their own with a baby who was often crying. Over 700 readers took part. Well over half felt sorry for the baby and 52% felt desperate. A quarter felt guilty and over a third felt depressed and angry. Many fathers felt sorrier for the baby than for the mother. The main causes of crying were thought to be hunger, pain and discomfort.

Over half the parents felt like smacking or shaking the baby but did not, and 10% of them admitted that they had smacked the baby on at least one occasion. Over a third shouted and screamed when the baby would not stop crying, and many mothers felt like crying themselves. Nine out of ten mothers cuddled or rocked the baby to try and stop the crying. Nearly half of the mothers sought help about the baby's crying, usually from their health visitor. Most parents felt unprepared for having a crying baby; four out of five mothers said the subject was never discussed at ante-natal classes. Out of the babies in this survey, 86% had stopped crying by the age of six months.

Another smaller survey published in *Community Outlook*[2] revealed an even more distressing picture about how the parents felt. Nearly all the mothers used words like guilt, failure, desperation, anger, resentfulness, confusion, shock, isolation, alarm, panic and monster. The baby failed to live up to expectations and some wished they had never had the child. The fathers did not express their feelings to the same extent, perhaps because they felt less deeply involved. Some admitted to feeling tired, desperate and helpless. A few also felt angry and violent. One-fifth of the fathers were concerned about the effects on their wives. In this survey, quite a number of parents actually resorted to shaking the baby and a few admitted to hitting the baby. Doctors say that shaking a baby violently can be very dangerous, causing possible brain haemorrhage.

In general, medical help left a lot to be desired, although prescribed drugs for the babies worked well in some cases. The recommendations of the survey were that doctors, midwives and health visitors needed better training in this field. It was clear that families needed help and they were not getting it. Self-help groups were recommended as the most acceptable kind of support.

Help for parents

Parents with crying babies can get support from many sources – their own family, friends, their health visitor or doctor (see Chapter 8 on getting medical help). For some, this is not always possible or not enough and they long to talk to someone else who has been through this experience and survived – someone who is just a parent like them and who can remain independent and anonymous to the family.

One evening in the autumn of 1981, a young mother gathered together a handful of other mothers, all with just one thing in common – a crying, sleepless baby. They set up a group called CRY-SIS (see Appendix 1 for address) and decided to help other parents going through the same problems.

CRY-SIS has now established a network of local contacts and groups throughout the country. The problem of a crying baby is nationwide. The group provides help on a one-to-one basis by a local volunteer who has had a crying baby too. Medical advice is not offered, but practical advice and support are given. Over these last few years, CRY-SIS has learned a great deal about the problems of crying babies by being in touch with hundreds of parents who have asked for help. These problems and how you can deal with them are described throughout the book.

The group works with doctors and health visitors, as well as other organisations offering help to parents and young children, like the National Childbirth Trust.[3] The need for CRY-SIS is becoming recognised and professionals are recommending this service to their parents and babies, often because they feel at a loss to help these families themselves.

My experience

When a friend asked me what I would call this book, I replied it could be 'Crying baby – how to cope.' My husband overheard the conversation and with a wry smile added 'But, we didn't cope!' I had no answer to that. Indeed we found it difficult to cope with our two crying babies. We muddled through from day to day in a haze of exhaustion and anxiety. We felt all the emotions discussed in this book; we experienced many of the problems. We had no magical solutions and little of the practical help since discovered and given here.

Some days were like a nightmare, and other days were tolerable. Some days were quite normal and if there were several in a row, we sighed with relief. Cruelly, they were often followed by several of the nightmare days – and so it went on. Gradually things improved. Now our children are five and three years old and our life together is much, much happier and easier.

Our first baby, Michelle, spent the first seven months crying a great deal. After birth, she slowly developed colic, at first in the evenings, but by six weeks old, she was screaming after every feed of the day. She improved a little after five months of age but never really cheered up until at seven months we discovered that she was allergic to cow's milk. She had been given supplementary bottle feeds from two weeks old, despite my wanting to fully breastfeed her. Most baby's formulas are based on cow's milk, a food known to cause allergic reactions in some children. Life was much happier for her once we changed her formula to a soya-based one. She became the baby we had always hoped for. However, poor Michelle was to suffer many other allergy problems over the next few years – eczema, asthma, diarrhoea, tantrums and sleep disturbances. Now at the age of five, she is a delightful, normal and healthy little girl.

Our second crier, Daniel, was born when Michelle was two and a half years old. From day one in hospital, he was screaming most of the day and sleeping very little. He was the sort of baby who was banished to the nursery every night as he kept all the others (and the mothers) awake! I remember one of the nurses asking me 'What will you do with this baby when you get home?' Needless to say, I had no idea! But I was determined to breastfeed, hoping to avoid allergies with this baby, and I had a few things up my sleeve from past experience. Daniel's continual crying and frequent breastfeeding went on until he was around three months old, when fortunately he suddenly started getting much better, crying less and going longer between feeds, although he still brought back milk after feeds until he was nine months old. We never really discovered why he cried so much, despite being admitted into hospital at one stage. He appeared healthy and gained weight well. I cut out cow's milk from my diet for a couple of weeks but there was no improvement to his crying (cow's milk protein can be passed through the breastmilk upsetting allergic babies). That crying baby turned into a calm and easy toddler, very confident and happy.

Parents' experiences

The often painful experience of parents and how they dealt with their crying babies are described throughout this book. They come from letters responding to appeals in several journals and newsletters.[4] Parents were invited to write about their experience of a crying baby. Fifty-nine mothers (some of who had had more than one crying baby) wrote, as well as one father and one midwife. Altogether, 63 babies were described, 30 boys and 33 girls. Forty-six were first babies, 12 second babies, two third babies and one fourth baby. Well over half the babies started crying within the first week of birth and half had stopped by six months. However, 25 babies still cried excessively at nine months of age and older. A summary including the duration of crying and what helped the babies and mothers can be seen in Appendix 3.

Many mothers said they had suffered from extreme exhaustion and many described depression, isolation and loneliness, both at the time and sometimes continuing for a long time afterwards. Few parents could leave their babies to cry for long. Most of the babies needed to be comforted a great deal and breastfed babies were put to the breast continually, although a few parents described their babies as being 'uncuddly' and felt they rejected their parents. One mother complained 'Baby books said things like "your baby will enjoy sitting in a bouncing cradle watching you work" and "string toys across the cot for him to look at". I wondered if I was living on a different planet.'

Some of these parents' experiences were quite devastating and probably not representative of the vast majority of parents with an irritable baby. Perhaps this is why these parents felt motivated to write – because it had been so awful. Please bear this in mind. There are degrees of the same problem and some of these cases represent what can happen at the worst end of the scale. However, although the intensity of the problem is not the same for everyone, the feelings and difficulties are shared by many.

Babies' needs

Crying babies are using the most powerful signal of distress that we know. They are crying out for HELP. They are using a mechanism which has ensured that babies survive. Babies are helpless and defenceless – they are very vulnerable. They rely solely on adults for their needs.

As one mother put it 'The mother's instinct is the least emphasised fact.' Your natural instinct will guide you if you let it but you may need a change of attitude to help you. For example, if you want to carry and comfort the baby, because you feel sorry for the child and cannot stand the sound of continual crying, do this without recrimination and accept it. Do not allow yourself to be intimidated by other people's remarks or advice to the contrary.

Liz felt this conflict but handled it in her own way. She writes 'My own health visitor said "Leave him to cry – he will soon stop it once he realises that you will not pick him up". I tried just leaving him but I defy anyone to listen to a baby cry all day seven days a week.' She went on to say 'I felt so guilty that I tried leaving him and again he started crying. I nearly hit him. Fortunately, I picked him up, but I was torn in two. Was I really spoiling him (as I had been told) or should I let him cry and constantly resent him to the point of physically hurting him? I decided that if indeed I was spoiling him it was better for my sanity than letting him cry.'

In 1979 an article in an American journal called 'Human care; cache or carry?'[5] observed that the young of animals fell into one category or another: either they were meant to be left for long periods in the 'nest' whilst their parents hunted for food (cache), or they were meant to be carried with their parents all the time whilst the parents were hunting (carry). The authors of the article concluded that human young definitely fell into the 'carry' category. They based their conclusions on several biological facts about babies. Firstly, human breastmilk, with its comparatively low protein content compared with other mammals, indicates that babies *should* be fed frequently, e.g. as newborns, every two to three hours. Also, a baby has natural reflexes which represent clinging and attaching himself to his mother. It also said that it seemed *natural* to carry babies as parents had carried them for hundreds of thousands of years, and only in the last hundred years or so had it become customary in Western society to leave babies in prams and cots. In non-Western societies today, babies are often still carried or held most of the time, even whilst their carers work, and they sleep next to their mothers, frequently suckling during the night. It is very rare for babies from these societies to cry at all, and if they do, it is treated with urgency as a matter of distress.

That is as may be, but for the majority of us, living in our society means leaving the baby to sleep alone and expecting some peace. But it may be helpful to bear in mind what happens elsewhere in the world and perhaps what Nature intended. It may certainly help if you are feeling guilty about carrying the baby around a great deal. Don't feel guilty about it. You cannot spoil your baby – although some people, like mothers and mothers-in-law may tell you that you can or you are making a rod for your own back.

If you need to get on with something else, like seeing to another child or preparing a meal, put the baby down and do not feel guilty if the baby is still crying. Also if the baby will not be comforted on this occasion by carrying and rocking and you have ruled out other possibilities, like hunger or wet nappy, put the baby down and go out of the room if you start feeling angry towards him or her. Have a break and a cup of coffee and go back when you feel calmer.

If you were living in another society, someone else might be at hand to hold the baby or see to the other chores for you. But as you are almost certainly on your own much of the time, it is not always practical to drop everything every time the baby cries. It is worth considering too that some babies need to cry themselves to sleep – they are not distressed, just tired.

What is important is that you respond *sensitively* to your baby and promptly if you can, so that the baby gets to know that you are there if needed. Handle the baby smoothly and with confidence too, so that he or she is not startled and feels at ease in your arms.

Crying in babies is not seen by researchers as 'goal-orientated' during the first six months – this means that babies cry because of a need inside that cannot be controlled, not because babies want to drive you to distraction or to assert their personality on you, although it often seems like it at the time!

Two researchers during the 1970s found some interesting information about mothers' responsiveness to their young babies.[6] They discovered that those mothers who responded promptly and sensitively to their babies' crying during the first six months were rewarded with babies who at the age of one, cried less than average, were more sociable and confident. Your extra attention and tender loving care will pay dividends in the long run.

Don't blame the baby

Remember above all that it is not the baby's fault – it is an unfortunate situation for both of you. It has been suggested that babies should be born a few months later than they are because their bodies need to catch up on so much important development during the first few months of life. Unfortunately, the baby's head would not be able to pass through the birth canal if he appeared any later – and what mother relishes the idea of another few months of pregnancy!

It is important to remember how immature babies are at birth, as it can help you understand their disruptive behaviour. Clearly, many fussy babies are at odds with the world into which they are born. They seem to feel discomfort, insecurity and be overwhelmed by stimulation from their new surroundings.

Beware of seeing your crying baby only negatively. It is easy to think of him or her as a 'monster' and negative comments about the baby can often come from other sources, like in hospital where nurses may say 'He is a naughty boy, isn't he?' or 'He won't give his mum any peace' or 'She will have you running to her ever time she cries. She'll soon have you wound around her little finger . . .'

Many loving parents come close to hurting their babies and feel terribly guilty – not because they harmed the baby but because they *felt* like doing it. These feelings at times of enormous stress and emotional upheaval are normal. You may feel anger, resentment and even aversion to the baby's cries but think of your baby as a sensitive being with very special needs and above all he or she needs you!

Notes

1 *Why do babies cry?* Sheila Kitzinger, Parents Magazine special report, March 1985.

2 *Frustration and despair.* Frances Kevill and Dr. Patricia Mortimer, Consultant Paediatrician at Chase Farm Hospital, Enfield, Middx. Community Outlook section of Nursing Times, May 1985.

3 National Childbirth Trust is an organisation which promotes a better understanding and care for childbirth and wishes to ensure that women can make informed choices (see Appendix 1 for address).

4 Appeals for parents' contributions appeared in *Parents, Mother,* and *Mother and Baby*, and in the newsletter of organisations like CRY-SIS, the National Childbirth Trust, La Leche League (breastfeeding support group), and the Hyperactive Children's Support Group (see Appendix 1 for addresses of these organisations).

5 Infant care: cache or carry? B. Lozoff and G. Brittenham. Journal of Paediatrics, 1979, 95, 478–483.

6 *Infant crying and maternal responsiveness.* S.M. Bell and M.D.S. Ainsworth. Child Development, 1972, 42, 1171–1190.

2

What is a crying baby?

If you feel your baby cries a great deal, then you have a crying baby. You may find a solution to the crying or ways of helping your baby cry less, but for the moment, accept that crying is *normal* for your baby. Reassure yourself too that it is not your fault.

All babies cry sometimes during the day, usually through hunger. It is surprising how the crying mounts up. Studies have shown that babies cry on average about two hours a day until they reach around six weeks of age; then crying usually decreases until around 12 weeks when they cry about one hour a day. However, there are vast differences amongst these babies, from those six week old infants who cry for less than one hour a day to those who cry for four hours or more a day. In general, there is little difference between the amount of crying of boy and girl babies.

Actually putting an amount on the crying of your baby does not always give an accurate picture of how irritable the baby is. For one thing, a crying baby has good days and bad days. For another, the amount of crying may not be very much – it often seems more than it is – because you are not *letting* the baby cry. You are picking the baby up and providing comfort to stop the crying. The problem is that as soon as you try to put the baby down to get on with something else, the crying immediately resumes.

Juliet described this problem and how she had to carry her baby constantly. 'The stimulation of looking at things seemed to distract her from crying,' she writes. 'I seemed to be stimulating her all the time to prevent there being any space in her life when she might cry.'

Typical patterns of crying

Babies develop cycles of sleep, wakefulness and crying. For most babies, sleep and wakefulness are the major cycles and crying only plays a minor part. But for difficult babies, crying often develops into a major part. There are certain types of criers and you may find that your baby fits into one of these typical patterns.

The early crier starts crying soon after birth. Alison had an early crier. She writes 'In the post-natal ward I was the only mother up pacing the floors long into the night. Sleep came to both of us only when I breastfed her in bed and kept her cuddled close. And so began many weeks of crying.'

The colicky baby usually cries after feeds and often in the evening, as if suffering from tummy ache. The baby can start crying from birth but more usually starts crying after a couple of weeks, often coinciding with your first week at home from hospital. (See section on colic, page 31).

Jane had a colicky crier. The pattern of crying initially was between 10.00 p.m. and 2.30 a.m. Jane continues 'Gradually, the crying started earlier and earlier. By ten days, it was early evening until about 2.30 a.m.; then it was all afternoon, evening and night until 2.30 a.m. At her worst, which was around three, four and five weeks, the crying and inability to settle to sleep for more than five to ten minutes, would start at 9.00 or 10.00 a.m., continue all day until about 2.30 a.m. At this time, which seemed to trigger off some inner response, she would finally sleep, solidly without waking until 9.00 a.m. the next morning. And then we'd be in for another 18 hours or so of hell and misery.'

The social crier wants to join in with the family and resents being left alone or shut away in a room. This baby thrives on attention and responds well to being cuddled and talked to. The baby's temperament improves with increased ability to join in social interaction, like reciprocal smiling with parents.

The frustrated crier is a strong hearty crier who seems generally irritable and frustrated by the confines of a baby's body. Melanie seemed to have a frustrated crier. 'There was no actual pattern to the crying. It was erratic and the force of the cry was very distressing and put a lot of strain on my husband and myself. The baby is very bright and is always one step ahead. She is a very demanding baby but much better now she is mobile.'

The older crier is more unusual – the baby who starts crying excessively at around five to six months of age when previously content. Teething may set off the crying and become a habit or it may coincide with the introduction of cow's milk or other foods to the baby's diet, in which case, food allergies should be considered. (See page 38).

The long-term crier may start off as one of the other crying types but it seems to develop into a way of life for this baby. The long-term crier may be helped by changes in the way the mother handles the baby, particularly if sleeping is poor. In fact, the problem may be due to lack of sufficient unbroken sleep and once the baby sleeps better, the baby becomes more content. The long-term crier may have an underlying cause, like allergy or infection and the crying is not likely to improve much until the condition is dealt with. The long-term crier may also be an intense baby who needs constant reassurance that you are still there. Ways of helping a long-term crier are described throughout this book.

Whatever type of crier you have, the crying is usually worst in the evening – just when you feel like resting after a busy day. One mother said that her baby's worst period of crying seemed to occur from 6.00 p.m. to midnight when the baby would drop off to sleep.

Any of the crying baby types can sleep well or sleep poorly. For instance, the baby may be miserable when awake during the day but have several good deep sleeps and may sleep reasonably well at night. On the other hand, the baby may sleep fitfully during the day for cat-naps of only minutes at a time and may sleep almost as little at night.

The babies in the *Parents Magazine* survey did most of their crying during the day. Two thirds of them were most unsettled during the evening. Nearly a quarter of the babies cried during the night. In this survey, most of the babies had stopped crying so much by the time they were six months old.

Over two-thirds of the 63 babies I received letters about started crying in the first week of life, and a further ten babies started crying between one and three weeks of age. Only seven babies started crying after three weeks old. Nearly half of the babies had stopped crying so much between three and six months but a depressing 25 babies were still crying after nine months of age. Over a third of the babies cried excessively for a period of between three and six months but about half of the babies cried for a period of six months or more. So much for any theory that babies stop crying at three months!

Crying – what it means

Every baby has its own repertoire of cries which are unique to that baby. Soon after your baby is born you will learn to recognise your own baby's cries. In time you will become more competent at interpreting what the crying sounds mean.

Sometimes, it is not easy to tell why your baby is crying. If this is the case, try to recognise different cry sounds in clear-cut situations, like when you know the baby is hungry or tired.

The hunger cry is more rhythmic than the other types of cry. The pain cry is sharp, loud and at a higher pitch, followed by a long pause before being resumed. There are other cries: the tired cry, the protest cry, the startle cry, the fever cry, the temper cry. John Kirkland, a cry researcher, suggests that it may be simpler for parents to think of cries on an intensity scale, e.g. low intensity cries could mean the baby is tired, medium intensity could mean hunger and high intensity pain.[1]

Researchers have analysed the features of different babies' cries and found that the cries of premature babies and babies with clinical abnormalities have unusual characteristics.[2] They have a higher or lower pitch than normal and are more urgent and irritating to the listener. Similarly, a baby who is ill usually produces abnormal cries. When the baby gets better, the cries return to a normal type of cry. Difficult babies have been found to have more arousing and irritating cries too.[3]

Crying is not the only form of communication that a baby uses either – other signals are facial expressions, eye contact and body movements, particularly of the arms and legs. To give you an example, if a baby has had too much of a certain stimulation, like being talked to by a visitor, the baby may cry, grimace, divert its eyes away and thrash about its arms and legs.

As well as the sound of the crying, parents use other information when deciding how to respond to their baby, like how long ago the baby was last fed. Becoming aware of all your baby's signals can help you too. Sometimes, recognising that the baby is diverting its eyes away or looking cross and intervening at this stage, can prevent a bout of crying. Maintaining eye contact with your baby can occasionally stop the baby slipping into the crying state.

Excessive crying does not seem to have any long-term ill effects on a baby. Many of the parents who wrote to me found their baby's temperament totally altered in time. Also, leaving a baby to cry occasionally is not dangerous unless the baby has a hernia or a severe heart disease. Check with your doctor to ensure that the baby does not suffer from any condition of this nature.

A common problem with crying babies is that it is difficult to tell when they are ill because they cry so much anyway. Watch out for any change in the amount of crying – either more or less – accompanied by changes in the types of cries you hear. Your instinct will usually tell you when something is wrong.

Notes
1 *Crying and babies. Helping families cope.* John Kirkland. Oxford University Press, 1985.
2 *Infant crying: theoretical and research perspectives.* Barry Lester. Plenum, 1985.
3 *The cries of infants of differing levels of perceived temperamental difficultness: acoustic properties and effects on listener.* Lounsbury, M.L. and Bates, J.E. Child Development, 1982, 53, 677–686.

3

Why do babies cry?

There are many reasons why a baby cries. To give you some idea of how complicated it can be, try to imagine yourself virtually paralysed and totally at the mercy of other people for your every need. You cannot communicate with the people caring for you, except by screaming out to convey messages of hunger, discomfort or disapproval. The people around you are speaking a language you cannot understand. You are bombarded by strange noises and smells. Faces hover over you and disappear from vision.

Can you imagine the frustration and how much you would appreciate comfort when it comes at last by cuddles and soothing noises. Looking at it this way, it is small wonder that babies do not cry more!

Most of the mothers in the *Parents Magazine* survey felt their babies cried because of hunger or discomfort. Younger and inexperienced mothers were more likely to see their babies' crying as a demand for attention or crying with no real cause. For most of the parents who took part in the Community Outlook survey, pain was thought to be the main reason for their babies crying so much.

There may be one cause for your baby's crying or there may be a combination of causes. It may just be that your baby is taking a while to settle down into the outside world.

The table opposite shows possible causes of crying. 'Personality' itself is not included. This is because it is not particularly helpful to think of your baby's personality as being the cause of incessant crying. It infers that the baby's personality is fixed and will not change. This is actually not true – babies' personalities often change and an irritable phase can be outgrown later. Rather than blaming the baby's personality, think of it this way. Your baby is crying because of something that upsets him or her – this is likely to be related to unpleasant stimulation from inside or outside the baby's body. That 'something' causes the baby to cry and to have certain personality traits. As soon as the 'something' improves or goes away, the crying will be reduced or cease and the baby's personality will change.

Babies do not need to cry to exercise their lungs either! If a baby is screaming, more air will be taken into the tummy and only cause more discomfort. Do not be too disappointed if you cannot find an obvious cause for your baby's crying. There are still ways you can help. Many parents never really discover why their baby cries so much. As one mother put it 'Friends used to ask me why he was crying and were amazed that I did not know the answer.'

Here are some of the common causes of crying.

Birth complications

Complications during pregnancy and during birth can account for a distressed and crying infant.[1] These complications include raised blood pressure, long labour, foetal distress, forceps delivery, and Caesarian section.

Drugs and anaesthesia during labour may affect the baby after birth – usually not immediately but after several days – causing excessive crying, sleeplessness and feeding problems. Epidurals have been found in some cases to be linked to a colicky jittery baby.[2]

Of course, not all difficult pregnancies and births result in a crying baby and not all crying babies have experienced a difficult birth. Out of 59 mothers who wrote to me, 19 reported pregnancy or obstetric complications.

Possible causes of babies crying

Birth complications	Infection and illness
Immaturity	Physical abnormalities
Colic	Pain or physical discomfort
Hunger	Fussing over the baby
Low sensory threshold	Allergies
Frustration and boredom	Effects of drugs

Maggie described her experience. 'Natalie was born after a very long and difficult forceps delivery. My pregnancy had been unpleasant and the labour horrific, a nightmare from start to finish. I had numerous complications and was left after delivery totally exhausted and in need of surgery to repair the damage.' Maggie went on 'I was physically in very poor condition, unable to cope with even basic chores such as nappy changing and suffering extreme discomfort in order to sit up to feed the baby. So passed the first 24 hours – both of us well doped with Pethidine. Then the screaming began.'

Maggie's experience is also a reminder of the exhaustion, pain and discomfort felt by many mothers after childbirth. 'Not a good start to our relationship' as she put it.

Immaturity

Some studies show that excessive crying is higher amongst premature babies than full-term ones.[3]

A pre-term baby may have experienced birth complications and is likely to spend a while in a special care unit. To start with, the baby may cry infrequently, if at all, because the baby is too immature and weak to cry. Fussiness usually starts between 33 and 35 weeks gestational age when the cry may sound shrill and distressing. From about 36 weeks, crying can be more lusty and come as a shock to the parents. The baby's earlier immature cry usually develops into a normal cry at around full-term age of 40 weeks.

When parents finally take the baby home from hospital, they often feel lacking in confidence and still worried about the baby's health, particularly if the baby cries a great deal. However, this is probably just part of normal development for this baby. Crying premature babies usually thrive and grow into healthy older babies.

If your baby was born premature and is crying excessively, mention this at subsequent check-ups at the hospital or to your health visitor. You will probably be reassured that all is well. You can use all the practical advice in this book to help you cope better and here are a few extra pieces of advice.

It is easy to become regimented by the routine of feeding in hospital. When you get home with the baby, you will find that there is no natural routine and the baby may want feeding more than three or four hourly. Incubators are bright and noisy – remember that your baby will not have been subjected to the normal environment of night and day. It will take a while for your baby to establish a daily rhythm of being more awake during the day and more asleep during the night. Also, if you are using 'womb music' tapes to soothe your baby, you will have to turn up the volume as premature babies only respond to higher levels of noise. Tapes of 'womb music' are described on page 68).

Christine experienced the problems of a crying premature baby. She had complications during her pregnancy and her baby, Amy, was born a month premature. Christine could not even hold her baby for the first five days, except for feeding, as she was in an incubator. When finally Christine took Amy home she thought all their troubles were over. 'It was such a relief to be allowed home but we didn't contemplate that our tiny baby could be so mentally destructive.' Amy started crying! On top of everything else, it can be a bitter blow.

Hunger

Hunger is often blamed for a baby crying continually. However, it can be difficult to know if a crying baby is really hungry. Many babies are difficult feeders and only want small amounts of milk at a time but frequently.

Crying babies are often awake for much of the time and are quite happy to take another feed a couple of hours after the previous one. They may be hungry or just want to suck for comfort. On top of this, crying babies tend to be always sucking on their fists, fingers or a dummy – this can be an indication of hunger or it can just be the baby's inherent desire to suck.

Many of the parents who took part in the *Parents Magazine* survey thought their babies were hungry. A crying baby advisory service set up by health visitors in Plymouth for six months found that 69% of calls for help were from parents worried about feeding problems.[4]

If you are breastfeeding, it is particularly easy to assume that your crying baby must be hungry and not getting enough breastmilk from you. To ensure that the baby is getting enough take the baby to the health clinic regularly and keep a close check on weight gain – normally a baby should gain between four and eight ounces a week, but many healthy and well-fed babies fluctuate in their weight gain, some weeks only gaining one or two ounces and others six ounces or more. Most babies double their birth weight by the age of six months.

If the weight gain is consistently poor and you are breastfeeding, the answer is to feed more frequently. If the baby is only having five or six feeds a day, try and increase it to eight or ten feeds. An indication that the baby is not getting enough milk would be dry nappies at changing times and scanty greenish stools. If the baby's nappies are always wet and the stools soft and yellowish, the baby is probably getting enough. You may be advised to give supplementary bottles of formula milk, but think carefully before doing this. Supplementary bottles interfere with the demand and supply system which operates in breastfeeding.

If the weight gain is satisfactory try not to be influenced by opinion that the baby would improve on formula feeds. Thirteen mothers who wrote to me gave up breastfeeding during the first few weeks often on the advice of their health visitor or GP. However, all the babies except one were just as bad or worse on formula milk.

Poor advice in hospital or at home about feeding schedules for breastfed babies causes many problems. Feed your baby on demand and be guided by your own judgement that the baby needs feeding. Liz found this problem when she was trying to establish breastfeeding her first baby. The nurses told her in hospital that the baby should go three to four hours between feeds. Liz felt that her baby cried for hours because he was hungry. She went on to have another baby but this time 'Instead of doing what the staff said, I fed her as and when she wanted it – about every two hours. Within a few weeks, she could go three to four hours. She never established a crying pattern and has been the most cheerful little thing going.'

If you are bottlefeeding, try offering bottles more often if you think the baby is still hungry. Make up each bottle as normal for the age and weight of the baby and offer a bottle every two or three hours. If hunger is the cause of the crying, the baby will take all the bottle and you will probably find that after two or three days, the baby is more settled and happy to go for longer intervals again. On the other hand, the baby may be more settled taking less formula milk but more frequently. Never reheat half finished bottles. It is important to ensure that the baby is getting every day the total correct amount of milk for his size and age – check with your health visitor and on the labels of the formula milk tins.

Babies have growth spurts, particularly at six and 12 weeks, when they are unsettled and seem constantly hungry for a few days. Frequent breastfeeding or extra bottles should ensure that you keep pace with the baby's demands.

Whether you are breast or bottlefeeding, do not be tempted to start the baby on solids early. The baby's delicate intestines cannot cope with anything but milk before three months and it is known that earlier introduction of solid foods can cause problems.

Kim wrote about her crying baby who her health visitor suggested weaning on to other foods at three months as she suspected hunger. Kim writes 'We'd already tried every milk on the market but to no avail. Weaning had no effect either.'

Do not forget that the baby may be thirsty instead of hungry every time, so try offering plain boiled water between feeds.

Colic

Excessive crying is often attributed to colic. But what is colic? A friend of mind, whose doctor diagnosed colic as being the cause of her baby's crying, rushed home from the surgery to thumb frantically through the index of her babycare book. She had never heard of it before and wondered if it could be something serious.

Colic is a condition which involves bouts of crying with what appears to be tummy pain. It is often accompanied by excessive gas or wind, which rumbles around the baby's tummy and provides temporary relief when passed up or down.

Colicky babies are tense and rigid during colic spells; pulling their legs up and going red in the face, they explode into inconsolable screaming. These spells of screaming continue on and off for anything from a few minutes to several hours, often ending in the baby falling into an exhausted deep sleep.

Colic usually occurs in the late afternoon and evening, often starting just after or even during a feed, although it can occur at other times during the day, and in severe cases will follow every feed of the day.

It is pitiful and distressing for the parents trying to comfort the baby who is struggling with pain and writhing in their arms. Little seems to work to pacify the baby for long. Feeding a colicky baby can be difficult too, as the baby tends to fight the breast or bottle. The baby seems hungry but cannot tolerate the milk entering its stomach. Mothers end up feeling unsure if the baby is still hungry or had too much.

However, colicky babies are normally healthy, thriving, gaining weight well and well-managed by their parents. Around 20% of babies suffer from colic at some stage. It usually develops in the first three weeks of life and clears up by 12 weeks, but it can go on up to four or five months of age, or occasionally even longer.

No-one really knows for certain what causes colic. One theory is that breastfed babies – who are notoriously unsettled in the evenings during the first few weeks – may be hungry, unsatisfied by the mother's milk supply which is prone to diminish by the early evening. Even poor positioning at the breast can prevent the baby getting enough milk at each feed and so by the evening the baby may be ravenous.

If hunger were the cause of colic, why does it occur equally with bottlefed babies, also predominantly in the evening? Some people feel that colic is caused by excessive sucking for milk and swallowing large amounts of air during feeding. However, X-ray studies of babies during colic spells do not show an excessive build-up of gas in the intestines. Dr. Illingworth, an eminent specialist, wrote about 'Three month colic' in 1954[5] and concluded that the most likely explanation was a localised obstruction of the passage of gas in the colon by spasm or kinking. It is possible that what gas is present in the colon gets temporarily trapped and causes discomfort until it frees itself.

There are some other theories about colic. Some researchers feel that colic is a phase of biological development for some babies. During the first few months, the functions of the baby's body are still maturing. The digestive system and the central nervous system, which controls the movements of the digestive tract, in some babies could not be functioning properly. It could be that the milk – either breast or bottle – is not broken down properly because of lack of enzymes, or it could be that the movements of the digestive system cause discomfort to an immature nervous system, or that the nervous system is not sending correct signals to the intestines. In support of the theory of colic being part of biological development, one research paper describes the usual onset of colic in premature babies as being within two weeks of the *expected* date of birth regardless of when the baby was actually born.[6]

Another paper in the 1960s proposed a relationship between colic and low levels of the hormone, progesterone, which affects smooth muscle activity and sleep patterns.[7] Colicky babies in this study were found to have low amounts of progesterone in their bodies or none at all, whereas non-colic babies had normal amounts of the hormone. It is suggested that there may be a lag between the birth and the colicky baby's own production of progesterone, and in the meantime the movements of the intestines are not as smooth as they should be, causing discomfort or pain.

Another theory is that some babies have a low sensory threshold (see page 34) and the build-up of stimulation during the day results in evening crying and letting off steam, when it is thought that the baby is trying to shut out completely all forms of stimulation.

Allergies, particularly to cow's milk protein, are known to cause colic symptoms (see section on allergies, page 38). Similarly, infections and some physical abnormalities can cause colic symptoms. It is therefore very important to have your baby checked by your GP to exclude these possibilities.

Theories regarding family tension or parental anxiety causing colic have been put forward in the past and have been largely discredited as there is no consistent evidence to support them. If parental anxiety were the cause of colic, it would probably be more common amongst the babies of first-time parents who are usually less confident and more concerned. However, colic is not a phenomenon of first babies – it can occur in any baby, irrespective of position in the family.

Coping with colic is frustrating and bewildering for the parents. As Ruth put it 'Colic was the diagnosis. "Oh, so what is the remedy?" I naively asked. "Nothing" came the supremely helpful reply from the doctor.'

The way to cope with colic is to first work out what kind of baby you think you have, e.g. baby with a low sensory threshold, hungry baby, allergic baby. If you are not sure you should seek advice from your health visitor or GP. You may then have to try out a few ways of coping. How to help your baby is described in Chapter 5. And to make life easier for you, the parent, help yourself by using the tips and advice given in Chapter 7.

Low sensory threshold

Standard tests of newborn babies find that a minority of them are tense and easily startled. They change their state rapidly, e.g. from sleep to crying, and they tend to thrash their legs and arms about more than normal. They have often endured distress during birth or pregnancy.

These babies have a low sensory threshold and are easily overwhelmed by stimulation both from outside and from within their bodies, including noise (e.g. traffic noise, children prattling, adults talking, radio or television – a combination of noise we take for granted), eye contact with other people, light (e.g. changes of light, faces coming and going), skin contact (e.g. clothes and nappies being changed, changes of temperature), smells (e.g. perfumes, cooking, smoke), movement (e.g. being jiggled, carried in a sling which they may hate), and being picked up and held. These babies are terrified of being dropped and often fling their arms and heads back when being picked up. Sensations from their own bodies include the movements of legs and arms, movements of food in the intestines, passing urine and stools.

The baby with low sensory threshold may be a poor comfort sucker, e.g. on a dummy. The baby may also seem uncuddly, looking away from you or closing its eyes whilst feeding, and may seem more content being left on its own. It can be very upsetting for the parents, who may feel that the baby is rejecting them.

In fact, the baby is trying to tell you to reduce the number of messages that the baby's body is receiving at a time. For example, do not talk or stroke the baby while feeding. If you are talking to the baby, do not rock the baby at the same time. Be guided by what the baby can tolerate. Keep the environment quiet and relaxed. Stop everyone handling the baby and perhaps cut out visitors for the time being. A routine in the home with little changes often helps these babies.

To soothe the baby, try *gentle* rhythmic rocking or singing. Swaddling should be very effctive as it helps counteract stimulation from the baby's own body movements. Try to get the baby to take a dummy. (See Chapter 5 for further advice about helping the baby.) Take every opportunity during quiet alert moments to interact with the baby and your relationship should build up on mutual confidence. Stroking the baby or massage may help both of you. Avoid jiggling the baby and ensure that your handling is smooth, gentle and confident.

Crying, particularly in the evening, for these babies is probably due to an overload of sensations and information during the course of the day. Improvement often comes with maturation of the central nervous system at around three months, when there is an increased ability to handle information.

Frustration and boredom

In contrast to the baby who is easily over-stimulated is the baby who seems to thrive on attention and being active and gets easily bored and frustrated. The baby does not want to be left alone in a pram with the same old rattle for company. So let the baby explore by sight and sound, and later by touch and action.

Frustrated babies often sleep very little and race through the development stages. A baby like this may turn out to have a higher than average mental ability. Many of the 'frustrated' crying babies whose parents wrote to me grew into bright, intelligent children. Carol wrote about her three-year-old: 'She has an incredible imagination and the vocabulary of a child years older. She is learning the alphabet and can pick out letters from her books.'

Kay, who is now a grandmother, well remembered her first daughter who cried for the first seven months. She said 'Once my daughter started to take an interest in things, she seemed a lot better – maybe she was just bored. She is by far the brainiest of my four children and all her life has commanded more attention than any of the others.'

Parents of children with exceptional abilities often remember them to have been crying, sleepless babies and to have displayed frustrated behaviour in the early years. Gifted children are rare, so do not pin your hopes too high on your screaming baby becoming a genius – although the possibility of it may be some consolation at the time!

Infections and illness

A baby with an infection may be hot and sweaty (what crying baby isn't), may be pale, may be vomiting or have diarrhoea, and may well be off its feeds.

Colds and coughs can cause the baby general discomfort and difficulty with feeding. Nasal drops prescribed by the doctor or bought in the chemist and used just before feeds can provide temporary relief to blocked noses, but these should not be used for more than one to two days without medcal advice. Make sure that a breastfed baby's nose is clear of the breast whilst feeding – a more upright position for the baby may help. There are some menthol creams sold in chemist shops which relieve cold symptoms when rubbed into the baby's chest.

Thrush is an unpleasant infection which can be passed from the mother's nipples to the baby's mouth and back again. Sometimes, the mother's vagina and the baby's bottom are also infected. There will be white patches in the baby's mouth which do not wipe away. The mother's nipples will be itchy and sore. Thrush needs medical treatment.

Urinary tract infection may have no other symptoms than those which look like colic, i.e. intermittent screaming and pulling up the legs.[8] Pain may be associated with passing urine. A persistently colicky baby, who is perhaps also pale, should be checked for urinary tract infection, particularly if the crying prevails well after three months. One group of hospitals found that routine urine tests showed that over 30% of the crying babies admitted for observation had a urinary tract infection and once treated, the symptoms, including crying, cleared up.

Ear infections are common amongst babies. They do not necessarily pull at their ears, as you might imagine. They may have flushed faces and be generally miserable.

Diarrhoea – whether caused by an infection or a symptom of food allergy – can be very dangerous for a baby as it can cause rapid dehydration. If the baby is passing motions virtually all the time with no or little urine, and the baby's mouth is dry and breathing raspy, bundle the baby in a blanket and take him or her to your doctor or your hospital immediately.

Physical abnormalities

Babies born with physical or mental handicap may cry a great deal from the pain or discomfort of the condition. Serious conditions should be detected soon after birth by medical staff. It is important that families are given information about facilities and support available to help them cope with the baby's condition. Babies with cerebal palsy do not like to lie on their tummies. Your GP, hospital, health visitor or local library will have information about groups who can help you cope with a particular handicap.

Sometimes, less serious conditions are not recognised until later. Some deaf babies cry a great deal but deafness can go undetected for several months. If you suspect that your baby does not hear properly– perhaps is easily startled, does not respond to noises or does not make babbling sounds by six months – ask your GP or health visitor to check the baby's hearing. All babies should have a routine hearing test by the age of seven or eight months.

Excessive crying can sometimes be caused by a hernia (a ruptured muscle) in the baby's groin or in the scrotum of boys – particularly associated with an undescended testicle. Your GP would check for this, but if you find any unusual lump in this area, take the baby to your doctor.

Some babies who cry excessively have partial obstructions in the stomach, intestines or bowels, although these conditions are rare. The baby will scream with hunger or pain, be pale and vomit large amounts, sometimes projected across the room. Consult your GP if this happens.

Pain or physical discomfort

General discomfort or pain will cause crying. The list of possible causes is endless – wind, constipation, nappy rash, eczema, teething, clothing discomfort, being too cold or too hot.

Lynne thought teething might have been to blame for her baby's crying. She writes 'He had his first tooth at four months and seems to have great trouble cutting the others. When he is teething he refuses all food, will sometimes bring even juice back and has terrible wind. I know teething is blamed incorrectly for many things, but I wonder if

Tom was born teething, but as he was so little we put his cries down
to other things.'

Chapter 5 gives advice on helping a baby with pain or discomfort.

Fussing over the baby

A new baby arrives and there is much excitement amongst family and
friends, who are all anxious to visit, hold and admire the baby. The
parents themselves spend hours delighting over their creation and
may be reluctant to let the baby stay out of their arms. Fathers may
enthusiastically jiggle and kiss the baby. Mothers may continually
change the baby's clothes for the next round of visitors.

Some babies find all this attention and stimulation far too much.
They need quiet, relaxed periods with their parents in familiar
surroundings, and they need to be allowed to settle to sleep in a pram
or cot on their own, even if they cry for a few minutes. Excessive
rocking for these babies can cause over-stimulation.

Most babies want small naps and longer sleeps throughout the day
and it is unfair to keep disturbing this pattern to display the baby to
yet another visitor. So be firm and learn when to say 'no' to visitors or
dad throwing the baby in the air. It will not be long before your baby
will enjoy the fuss and squeal for more.

Allergies

Your baby's crying may be caused by an allergic reaction to food or
something in the environment. It is estimated that 12½% of the
population are atopic –that means they suffer from allergic reactions.
In babies and children, allergic reactions can include colic, crying,
sleeplessness, vomiting, diarrhoea, excessive wind, constipation, skin
rashes, eczema (dry, scaly skin which is itchy and can bleed), wheezy
chest, asthma, excessive dribbling, constant running nose (rhinitis),
headaches, behavioural problems, poor concentration and poor
coordination. Repeated middle ear infections and 'growing pains' in
the legs can also be linked with allergy.

If one parent is an allergy sufferer, perhaps having migraines, hay
fever, catarrh, or asthma, there is a 50% chance of an offspring being
atopic; if both parents are allergy sufferers, the chances are further

increased. It may be helpful to know this when considering the possibility of a baby being allergic. Not all allergic babies come from allergic families.

An allergic reaction is caused when a substance which is tolerated by most people enters the body and causes an over-reaction. It seems strange that the reaction to something eaten can result in a skin or other condition, but that is how the body may react. Doctors and other professionals often differentiate between allergies and intolerances. There may be subtle differences in diagnosis, but the effects are the same on the baby or child – an unpleasant reaction.

Suspicion of possible allergy is aroused if the baby is crying a great deal and there are other symptoms like the ones described. Twenty-three of the 63 babies whose parents wrote to me had allergies confirmed by their doctors and once the problem was sorted out the crying and sleeplessness improved greatly. It was not always easy for the parents to get help. As Sherriann, whose baby suffers from milk allergy, puts it 'We have only come as far with a great deal of persistence on my part and not without many comments from those in authority such as "He is just a difficult baby", "Does he meet many babies of his own age?", "Some babies just cry a lot".' She adds 'People often do not take allergies to food seriously.'

Cow's milk

The most common substance which upsets babies is cow's milk – either because of one of the milk proteins or the milk suger (lactose). This allergy is even more common in families of non-European origin, e.g. African and Chinese races who have not practised rearing cows and drinking the milk. Babies' formulas are normally based on cow's milk. If the baby is breastfed, one supplementary bottle of formula milk, perhaps given in hospital, could set up a cow's milk sensitivity. Babies can also react to cow's milk consumed by the mother and passed through the breastmilk to the baby, often causing colic symptoms. Recent research,[9] as well as many mothers own experiences, back this up.

The diagnosis and management of allergy should not be undertaken by the mother on her own, so if you suspect cow's milk allergy consult your GP or health visitor about this. It is not a good idea to keep switching brands of formula milk. Always seek medical advice first. Normally, there should be no reason why a baby should stop taking cow's milk formula for a while to see if it makes a difference to the crying and other symptoms. A bottlefed baby will usually be changed to soya-based formula milk which is available at chemists and can be obtained on prescription for diagnosed cow's milk allergy. The mother is also advised to keep the baby off all dairy products if the baby has already been weaned, including butter, whey, yoghurt, cheese, dairy icecream and dried baby foods containing milk. Sometimes it may be necessary to exclude beef.

The breastfeeding mother will be advised to omit cow's milk and other dairy products from her own diet and to substitute perhaps soya or goat's milk for drinks or in cooking. If the baby has begun eating other foods, all dairy produce should also be avoided. It is possible to buy margarines which do not contain any cow's milk from most supermarkets and health food shops (Tomor margarine is one brand). Check on the label that margarine and other foods, like biscuits, do not contain whey which is extracted from milk.

The baby who is reacting to cow's milk may become worse for a few days. This is a kind of withdrawal reaction, but thereafter things should improve considerably. It can take one to two weeks to see a definite improvement. Unfortunately, some babies are allergic to soya too.[10] Some tolerate it better than cow's milk but for a few babies, neither cow's milk nor soya are tolerated at all well. If the symptoms are severe and the baby is failing to thrive or at risk through illness, special formulas, like Pregestimil or Nutramigen, can be prescribed. These formulas are more likely to be acceptable to a highly allergic baby as the proteins and sugars are already broken down and easier for the baby to handle. They are not widely available, however, as they are very expensive.

Goat's milk is not suitable for babies under six months. It can be tried as an alternative to cow's milk for older babies, but the proteins in goat's milk are similar to those in cow's milk and often cause similar reactions. Fresh goat's milk should be boiled carefully before use to destroy any harmful bacteria. Vitamin supplements may be necessary too – discuss this with your GP, health visitor or hospital dietician. Vitamin supplements should not contain artificial colouring or preservatives. Other milks, like tinned evaporated milk, should not be given to a baby under six months as they are incomplete and unsuitable for babies.

If the baby improves when cow's milk is excluded from the diet, your GP will normally recommend that the baby be challenged after a few weeks or months with a very small amount of cow's milk formula. If the baby reacts again, you will usually be advised to try again in three to six months time. Sometimes, a short rest off cow's milk allows the body to recover from a temporary sensitivity following say an illness or infection. If this is the case, the parents should be aware that the child has a tendency to be sensitive to milk and possibly to other foods or additives, should other allergic symptoms like asthma or headaches develop at a later age.

It can come as quite a relief to the parents to find out that there is a cause to the baby's crying. My daughter suffered from colic and eczema as a baby. She improved dramatically once taken off cow's milk formula at the age of seven months, replaced by a soya formula. We tried reintroducing cow's milk on several occasions but without success, so she continued having rather large amounts of soya until at the age of three and a half, she became allergic to that too, developing asthma and becoming unwell. (Current opinion favours keeping the amount of soya substitute down to between a half to a pint a day once a baby has been weaned.)

After some months of ill health and asthma attacks, we consulted an allergy doctor who suggested a complete rest from soya, followed by a rotation diet of goat's milk, Carnation milk (often tolerated by milk-sensitive people), and soya milk – a different milk being used in rotation every day. Within a short time, the asthma, eczema and general ill health improved considerably. At this time and with the help of this doctor, we also discovered that Michelle was reacting to additives in foods, particularly certain artificial colourings, flavourings and preservatives. Her behaviour improved once these were excluded from her diet as far as possible. Now at the age of five, she tolerates cow's milk but still does not tolerate various food additives.

A breastfed baby known to be sensitive to cow's milk, or coming from an allergic family, should continue to breastfeed for drinks for as long as possible. It is a good idea to avoid introducing cow's milk to the diet before 12 months. Meanwhile breastmilk or soya milk formula can be used in cooking. Breastfeeding is important because it gives protection and immunities to help combat allergic reactions. Far fewer totally breastfed babies develop allergies and they are generally healthier and suffer from fewer infections. Many allergy experts recommend full breastfeeding with no supplementary bottles and nothing else except boiled water added to the diet for the first five to six months.

Reactions to foods

Babies can be allergic to other foods as well as cow's milk. When introducing other foods to the baby, these should be regarded as just tastes to start with. Make sure that you proceed slowly and carefully, introducing one food at a time. For example, apple means apple and not apple plus sugar plus custard. Start with simple fruits like bananas and pears (not citrus fruits at first), vegetables like potatoes and carrots, and cereals like baby rice (not wheat). Ask your health visitor's advice about weaning.

Some allergy experts recommend avoiding aluminium saucepans for cooking as aluminium deposits can seep into food. It is also a good idea to rinse washing up well to remove all traces of washing up liquid.

Manufactured babyfoods often contain a large number of ingredients. It is easy and cheap to make your own food, which can often fit in with family meals, e.g. a mashed banana or plain mashed potato. Beware gravy and custard powders which often contain colouring, flavour enhancers and preservatives. These additives will be listed as ingredients on labels and packaging and should be avoided by both the breastfeeding mother and baby. Some additives are not allowed in food intended for babies and young children in any case.

Babies' first drinks should be boiled water. Other drinks, including baby's blackcurrant and orange drinks, can cause problems because of the fruits they contain or the high levels of sugar. If water is not accepted, give pure fruit juices, like apple and pineapple juice, well-watered down with no added sugar. Avoid pure orange juice until the baby is older and introduce with care. Avoid giving squashes, sweets or shop-bought jellies, as these often contain food colourings, particularly tartrazine (E102) and sunset yellow (E110).

A breastfeeding mother investigating the possibility of allergy will be advised to look at her own diet carefully. Sometimes, the mother is drinking large quantities of coffee, tea or milk. Try cutting down or eliminating these one by one. If you drink squash use those which contain no artificial colouring, flavouring or preservatives.

Sometimes, the mother discovers she is eating a food which she is allergic to herself and it upsets the baby too. She may have cravings for this food, like chocolate or cheese, and feel unwell if she does without it. Try and cut out any foods which you eat in excess or which you crave, for your sake and the baby's. You may feel unwell for the first few days, but after a week or so, you may feel better than you have for a long time. On the other hand, you may be eating or drinking a food which you do not really like at all for the sake of a good diet, for instance cow's milk. Chances are you are allergic to it, so do not bother to eat any food that makes you feel ill or which you dislike.

Some foods to consider suspect apart from dairy produce are chocolate, eggs, wheat, and citrus fruits particularly oranges.

Problems with water

Tap water can prove a problem in some areas. Boiling tap water, which is recommended for babies in any case, often helps. A consultant paediatrician and allergy specialist who has undertaken studies of children suffering from allergies, has found a number of instances where the children's symptoms were aggravated by tap water, which can be recycled and contain many chemical compounds, in particular chlorine. This specialist suggests that a crying, sleepless baby could be taken off tap water for a few weeks, which should be substituted by boiled, bottled water – Malvern water or Highland Spring water are recommended, as these are not as high in mineral content as some others, which are considered unsuitable for babies. If there is a definite improvement, substantiated by challenge (trying tap water again to see if there is a deterioration), parents could consider purchasing a water filter, available from hardware shops and chemists. Some types will filter out fluoride too, if necessary, and some can be plumbed into the drinking water system. Filtered or bottled water could also be taken by the breastfeeding mother instead of tap water to see if this helps her baby's symptoms.

Several parents have found filtering water was beneficial for different types of allergic reactions, including colic and eczema. When using tap water, run the cold water tap for two or three minutes every morning before use, in case of build-up of deposits in the pipes.

Vitamin and fluoride supplements

Babies can sometimes be sensitive to vitamin supplements, like the drops sold in the clinics which often contain additives such as flavourings and preservatives. Some parents have reported that the baby's excessive crying or sleeplessness started with the introduction of these drops. Many breastfeeding experts do not feel that vitamin supplements are necessary for breastfed babies, providing the mother's diet is varied and nutritionally adequate. Vitamins are available in breastmilk and are very well utilised by the baby. However, in some cases mothers and babies may require extra vitamins, particularly dark-skinned people living in this country. These requirements should be discussed with your health visitor. Some breastfeeding mothers may find that taking a general vitamin and mineral supplement themselves, preferably one containing no additives, helps the baby.

Fluoride supplements are often recommended by dentists to reduce tooth decay, but fluoride can cause problems with allergic reaction, whether taken by the baby or the breastfeeding mother. If in doubt, remove it from the diet to see if this brings about an improvement. Fluoride drops, tablets, gels, disclosing tablets and toothpastes often contain additives – colouring, flavouring and preservatives. Ask your dentist and health visitor about the need for extra fluoride and appropriate sources, either dietary or in supplement form. Remember too that some areas of the country have higher levels of natural or added fluoride in the water supply than others, so supplements may be unnecessary. Your local Water Board will give you information about fluoride levels.

Good and bad days

Some days you may find that the baby reacts more severely to a food than other days, sometimes to only a small amount. Other days, tolerance levels are higher. This is because other factors may affect the baby's ability to handle sensitive substances. These factors include the baby's general health (eg colds or infections), stress levels (eg teething or getting highly excited), and environment. Babies can react to chemicals and pollutants in the atmosphere, including fumes, plastics, detergents, pollens and moulds.

Keep the environment in the home as natural and free from chemicals, perfumes, pesticides and sprays as possible. Keep pets away from the baby. Clean the baby's room regularly from accumulated dust. Bedclothing should be free from feathers. And don't smoke or let anyone else smoke near the baby.

It is a good idea to keep a diary of all foods and drinks consumed by the mother who is breastfeeding her baby, or eaten by the baby, and a description of the baby's symptoms, which you could rate on a 0 to five scale, 0 meaning no symptoms and five meaning severe symptoms. It is sometimes possible in this way to discover a food which is causing reactions or perhaps even several foods which might trigger different reactions. It is always useful to keep such a diary to discuss with your health visitor, GP or hospital.

If your child suffers from an allergy, it may be a short-term problem for a few weeks or months, or it may be a long-term problem, lasting for several years or even a life-time. Special diets are a nuisance and seem complicated at first, but with help and advice they do become easier to handle. There are some good books around on allergies and diets which will help you (see Appendix 2). If it seems a difficult allergy problem, ask your GP to refer you to an allergy specialist at a hospital. A hospital dietician can also help with advice on special diets and vitamin and mineral supplements, if necessary. There are allergy self-help groups now in most areas which can provide helpful practical information from sufferer to sufferer or parent to parent. Further details are in Appendix 1. See also section on the hyperactive child, page 125.

Effects of drugs

If you are breastfeeding your baby, consider any drugs you take, alcohol or the nicotine in cigarettes, as being possible antagonists, causing crying or other symptoms. Drugs include aspirin and other pain relievers, decongestants, cold remedies, laxatives, antibiotics and sleeping tablets. Always mention to your GP that you are breastfeeding if drugs are prescribed for you. The contraceptive pill can reduce a mother's breastmilk supply and has been known to cause the baby's rejection of the breast or undue fussiness.

Antibiotics and other medicines are often prescribed for crying or allergic babies (see page 120), but these can cause dramatic behavioural reactions, due either to the drug itself or to the colourings and flavourings often added to them. Ask your GP to prescribe medicine free from colouring and flavouring. Doctors may be cautious about prescribing repeated courses of antibiotics, which can affect the baby's gut lining and possibly cause sensitivity or allergy.

Anxiety in parents

It seems so unfair that parental anxiety is sometimes blamed for a baby crying excessively. True, some parents are naturally more anxious than others, or perhaps have experienced a miscarriage or other tragedy, making their baby feel very precious. True also that babies seem to pick up tension from the atmosphere, no doubt via raised or harsh voices, parents' tense, erratic handling and unrelaxed, stiff arms whilst holding them.

However, to blame already guiltridden parents for causing their crying baby is unrealistic in most cases, when it can happen just as easily to the most confident and relaxed parents, when it can happen to third-time parents, when one twin can be a crying baby and the other placid, and when other factors can be discovered, like infection, hernia or allergy.

It is after all a chicken and egg situation – the crying baby causes the tension and this probably causes the baby to cry more. You could well try and break into this difficult cycle by making an effort to stay calm, to respond appropriately to the baby, and to relax as much as possible. Using the practical advice in this book, you may find yourself winding down and the baby may respond too. The first step is to stop blaming yourself. It is *natural* to feel anxious about a crying baby. It is a sign of being a loving and caring parent. And almost certainly, the crying baby came first and your anxiety as a result of it.

Notes

1 *Comparison of mothers' with trained observers' reports of neonatal behavioral style.* Infant Behavior and Development, 1984, 7, 299–310. I. St. James-Roberts, D. Wolke.

2 *Effects of epidural anesthesia on newborns and their mothers.* A.D. Murray, M.R. Dolby, R.L. Nation, D.B. Thomas. Child Development, 1981, 52, 71–82.

3 *Mother-infant interaction in premature and full term infants.* J.W. Crawford. Child Development, 1982, 53, 957–962.

4 *A crying baby advisory service.* A. Bogie. Health Visitor, December 1981, Vol. 54, 535–537.

5 *'Three months' colic.* R.S. Illingworth. Archives of Disease in Childhood, 1954, 29, 165–174.

6 *Colic in low birth weight infants.* J.E. Meyer and M.M. Thaler. American Journal of Disease in Childhood, 1971, 122, 25–27.

7 *A study of the possible relationship of progesterone to colic.* R.L. Clark, F.M. Ganis and W.L. Bradford. Pediatrics, 1963, 65–71.

8 *Colic as the sole symptom of urinary tract infection in infants.* J.N.H. Du. Canadian Medical Association Journal, 1976, 115, 334–337.

9 *Cow's milk proteins cause colic in breastfed babies: a double-blind cross-over study.* I. Jakobsson and T. Lindberg. Pediatrics, 1983, 71, 268–9.

10 *Controlled trial of oligoantigenic treatment in the hyperkinetic syndrome.* J. Egger et al. The Lancet, March 1985, 540–545.

4

Crying baby in the family

A crying baby comes as quite a shock to parents and household. There is a terrifying sense of responsibility and the outlook may seem bleak.

Parents experience feelings of utter inadequacy, failure, helplessness and fear that all is not well. The emergence of intense and sometimes frightening emotions take parents by surprise, like the love/hate/guilt triangle described by one mother.

Parents often feel out of control of their lives and unable to function as they used to. This, together with noise of the crying and the demands of the baby, put a tremendous strain on the parents and their relationship. They can start blaming themselves and one another. Arguments and resentments can brew in the highly charged atmosphere. Jeanette describes this strain. 'My husband wasn't any help – it was "my job". At night he needed his sleep for work next day, and during the evening and weekend (when he wasn't working) he wanted some peace to unwind.'

Within a relationship, partners have different roles, which include those of lover, friend, mothering/fathering the other partner, being mothered/fathered by the other partner, and being a parent to the children. These roles receive quite a battering when there is a crying baby in the home.

Sexual relationships and social contact suffer. Alison describes what happened to her marriage. 'For a time, I forgot I was a wife as well, and our sex life was greatly affected. I was always too tired to bother. There was little chance to talk and be a couple as every evening Laura was with us. Our social life was non-existent – there was no way she could be left and anyway, she settled too late to go out. My husband was understanding to a point but he was not there often enough to appreciate the problem. Without any support the strain showed on me.'

The baby's demands take over the parents' ability to 'mother' or 'father' one another, just at a time when they need to be loved and reassured themselves. Looking after other children in the family becomes an added burden and source of guilt.

Parents find it difficult explaining their negative feelings to their family, friends, or professional advisors. They often feel they are not being taken seriously and some may clam up after a while, staying behind closed front doors, only to isolate themselves further. One mother describes this. 'It did not help that every time we went anywhere or had visitors the baby behaved immaculately and seemed to make a lie of my stories of non-stop crying.'

Relations and friends may live too far away to be able to offer practical help or may have their own commitments. Parents may not be used to asking for help, having previously led independent lives.

First-time parents with a crying baby are particularly vulnerable to stress, having no experience of parenting and often little contact with babies. Their confidence is delicate and easily shattered. First-time mothers find the transition into parenthood especially hard and may wish they had never had the baby, which seems to have ruined their lives. They have often had little opportunity to make friends with other mothers of young children and miss the social contacts, status and interest of their previous job. They may feel uncomfortable or strange in their new role as mother. Depression, isolation and despair can quickly set in. Some studies found that first-time parents respond to crying with greater arousal and more irritation than experienced or non-parents.[1]

The majority of parents who wrote to me were first-time parents – 46 out of 59. This may be an indication of the deep effect that a crying baby has on a first-time parent. It was obvious that their confidence had taken quite a knock but most of the mothers who had gone on to have subsequent children found their confidence restored.

Parents with other children may find their confidence higher, but if previous babies were not criers, they will find it just as hard to adapt to the new baby. Fifteen of the 63 babies in my survey were second or subsequent babies. Parents often described problems coping with the baby and the rest of the family.

Other children have to take a back seat and although they often survive the experience relatively unscathed, the mother feels guilty about the lack of time and energy she has for them. She may be irritable with older children and expect a great deal from them. Older children can start to resent the baby and cause trouble. On the other hand, a friend of mine found it helpful to commiserate with her two-year old toddler about how 'horrible' his little brother was.

Single-parents may find a crying baby most distressing of all, having no partner with whom to share their feelings and the practical care of the baby. They may have to accept more than anyone any offers of help and that putting the baby down to cry is a necessity at times. Donna was a single-parent and also had a two-and-a-half year old child. She writes 'I was very tired and mostly had to just leave her to cry, especially during the night. My mother helped a great deal.'

Unemployed fathers will create many social and financial pressures in the family. Fathers in this situation can at least take the opportunity to get to know the baby better than others who have less time at home, as well as to share with their partner the everyday care of the baby and any other children.

When the crying gets you down

If babies can be so different, then so can their parents. Whether your baby's crying gets you down, depends on your expectations, your experience with babies, and your tolerance levels. For example, one parent may find evening colic quite unbearable, disrupting as it does evening meal times and the opportunity to relax with their partner. Another parent can cheerfully cope with an irritable baby who cries for the best part of most days, but suddenly after a few weeks or months, finds the baby's crying overwhelming.

The ability to cope with a crying baby goes in phases too. Some days do not seem as bad as others even though the baby's behaviour is much the same. Outside influences and distractions often help you to cope better. Some days, you may just feel more tired or more tense than others.

People often wonder, including the mother herself, why so much time is taken up looking after a baby – why the breakfast things remain unwashed at 4.00 p.m. and why there is no sign of dinner at 8.00 p.m. Looking after an average baby is an eight-hour a day job. Just feeding, changing, winding, bathing, getting the baby off to sleep – all adds up. It is no wonder there is little time left for other jobs like housework, cooking, ironing, shopping, or seeing to other children. A crying baby means the amount of time seeing to the baby is more and the time left for other chores is less. It is hardly surprising that exhaustion can take over. One mother found she was 'physically and mentally exhausted'.

Mothers have been found in studies to be subject to physical stress upon hearing their own babies' crying, with increases in their heart rate.[2] Stress and exhaustion can produce physical symptoms and even depression. My stomach used to tighten into a knot when my babies started crying. Parents may find themselves actually feeling ill, or experiencing minor aches and pains, like headaches, palpitations or sweating.

Danger signs for the baby

A crying baby can produce intense feelings of anger and resentment in a parent. Sometimes, these feelings are vented against the baby. More than half of the parents who wrote to me came very close to hurting the baby.

Elaine wrote: 'The only way I managed to keep sane was to put her in one room – make sure she was safe. Then go into another room and relax with a cup of tea and the stereo earphones on so I did not hear the screams. Some people may think that that was cruel, but it was either that or else maybe me doing something to her, as I must admit I have come very close to violence.'

Serious child abuse is not very far away for many parents coping with a crying baby. Something inside them usually stops them from doing real harm.

Research studies into child abuse have indicated that a crying baby or a whining child was the main reason given for the parent hurting the baby or child, although complex factors, like social stress and isolation, also influenced the parents' actions.[3]

When researchers looked at child abusers' response to a baby crying, they found that the child abusers experienced great physical arousal. They reported more aversion and less sympathy to the crying. Researchers also found that parents who had hurt their children responded automatically to smiling *and* crying babies in the same way. It seemed that they wanted to switch off *any* signal from a baby.

Mothers of difficult temperament babies were also found to be less sensitive to changes in a baby's expressions, i.e. from crying to smiling or from smiling to crying.

It would seem that the stress of looking after a crying baby can make parents less receptive to the baby's signals. So, try and be aware of your baby's good moments as well as the more difficult times.

A mother's story

This is a story of a mother who had a crying baby. It is made sadder because the mother, Pauline, cannot have any more children due to health problems. Pauline had been repeatedly told she would always be childless. A miracle happened and she conceived, but there followed a threatened miscarriage, long stays in hospital and finally a Caesarian section. This is Pauline's story after the baby arrived.

'I felt numb. I was subdued and I felt ill. I wasn't able to breastfeed my baby but it didn't bother me. I wanted to be left alone. I was tired and weak – all I wanted to do was sleep. My visitors arrived over the next couple of days with beaming smiles and arms full of gifts for baby and myself . . . I felt nothing except fear that, even at this early stage, I wouldn't be able to cope. My baby cried and didn't sleep much. I was stuck in this room by myself, crying constantly and feeling so, so tired. Surely it wasn't supposed to be like this? Where were all those loving, protective feelings? What had I done to deserve this baby that cried all day and most of the night? The sister gave my baby a dummy – something which I didn't want for her. They said she was a windy, colicky baby and the dummy would comfort her. Nothing seemed to comfort her. If she wasn't crying, she was bringing all her feed back

. . . I felt as though the walls were closing in on me – I had to get out of that room.

'I begged and pleaded to be able to go home. Perhaps I would feel better in my own home and my baby would "settle down". At last, I was to be discharged. The midwife would come every day to advise and help me. There was snow on the ground and it was bitterly cold. I arrived home to a new pram with matching carrycot, sterilising unit – in fact, just about everything a new Mum could wish for. Why didn't I feel on top of the world? My husband had saved all his holidays and was to have six weeks at home with me and our baby – just until I got back on my feet. Would I ever get back on my feet? We sterilised bottles, we made up feeds, we had slow teats, medium teats, we had fast teats. We bought disposable nappies and had special cream on prescription because she was very prone to nappy rash. She was definitely a colicky baby according to the midwife. So we had medicine on prescription for her. It helped just a little.

'She cried and rarely slept. I grew more and more depressed, tired and weary. I slopped around in housecoat and slippers – I couldn't even be bothered to get dressed. Anyway, the snow was thick on the ground and it was so cold. I wouldn't be able to go out for weeks. Christmas and New Year came and went without my hardly noticing. The midwife had ceased her daily visits and my husband was due back in work. I would be alone all day, with this baby that did nothing but cry and "throw up" all over the place. I was terrified.

'The first week I cried all day with her. I just wasn't meant to be a Mum. I had no maternal instincts and my baby hated me. Whatever was I going to do? The health visitor came – a spinster in her forties at least – she said my baby wasn't gaining weight as she should, she was underfed, I wasn't holding the bottle right – in fact, I wasn't doing anything right, at least not according to her text book. I would have to go back to see the consultant paediatrician. My husband and I took Kellie every week for months whilst a close check was kept on her weight etc. There was absolutely nothing wrong with her.

'I was still very tired and weary and the sleepless nights and constant crying were now beginning to get to my husband. Whenever he phoned, I would be crying and it was still an effort just to get dressed and go to the corner shop.

'My baby was now four and half months old. We still hadn't had a single night's sleep and giving her a bottle was a nightmare in itself. She would take approximately two ounces over the period of an hour and a half. My husband had gone to work and it was pouring with rain, cold and very windy. I was desperate. I just could not stand another day with this crying baby. I wrapped her up, put her in her pram and walked the streets. I found myself in the local park which was utterly deserted. I was soaking wet through, weary and honestly just wanted to close my eyes and never open them again. If I left the pram in the park, would it be traced back to me? Could I just walk away and pretend I never had a baby? Somebody please help me!

'The clinic was round the corner. I would take her there and leave her. I stumbled into the clinic and fell into the arms of the clinic paediatrician, weeping profusely. I begged her to take my baby away. I was at the end of my tether and didn't even want to make the effort to cope. I just wanted to go home and leave the responsibility of my baby to anyone who would have her. I was given a strong hot cup of tea and the paediatrician soothed my baby. Why wasn't I able to do that? My baby really must hate me. I was given a prescription for a mild sedative for myself and for a sleeping draught for my baby. There would be no follow-up – I really must try and pull myself together, as there was absolutely nothing wrong with my baby.

'We gave her the sleeping draught that night and I took the tablets. She slept intermittently and was wide-eyed and yelling at 6.00 a.m. We decided that the sleeping draught did work in part, but because even at such a tender age, she tried to fight it, it left her with a massive "hangover". The following day she was more crochety than ever. Still, for the sake of a few hours unbroken sleep every night we decided to persevere with the sleeping draught knowing the following day would be hell. When my baby did sleep for a short time, I would look at her with an overwhelming feeling of love, mingled with hate. I had wanted her so much. My life would be complete with a baby girl all of my own and all she had done was reduce me to a mental and physical wreck.

'Our social life was non-existent and we had neither the opportunity, energy nor inclination for sex. We didn't even have the energy for decent conversation for most of the time. Routine housework went right out of the window. Clothes were ironed minutes before they were put on and dust could be seen on my skirting board. I had so much wanted to be the perfect wife and mother – was there such a thing? My husband was now really beginning to feel the strain of endless sleepless nights, working six days a week and a wife who was constantly tired and depressed. Still he remained very supportive, although there was a definite gulf between us. Who said a baby complemented a marriage?'

Kellie continued with her poor sleeping but gradually cried less during the day. Pauline asked for help with her depression and her GP referred her to a psychiatrist who she went to see every week for eight months, although Pauline did not feel that it helped her.

Kellie seemed to prefer her daddy and Pauline felt shut out of their good relationship together. The child would also not go to anyone else but her parents and close family. Pauline discovered her daughter was allergic to cow's milk and once on a diet free of dairy produce, Kellie's health and behaviour improved considerably. Finally, Kellie started playschool and Pauline joined its committee to help run it. Both made lots of friends. Kellie loved playschool and was a bright child.

Pauline ends her story on this reflection. 'It would have been easier maybe if I had had someone to talk to who had experienced a crying, sleepless baby and was actually willing to admit it, who would listen whilst I poured out my fears, feelings and grief, and who would understand just how I was feeling and could maybe offer practical help. Through my experiences, and there have been so very many, I feel that I am now able to help others with similar problems.' Pauline joined CRY-SIS, the support group for parents with crying babies, and is one of the contacts helping other parents in her area.

Notes
1 *Adult physiological response to infant cries: effects of temperament of infant, parental status and gender.* C.F.Z. Boukydis and R. Burgess. Child Development, 1982, 53, 1291–1298.
2 *Differential parental response to familiar and unfamiliar infant distress signals.* A.R. Wiesenfeld, C.Z. Maletesta, and L.L. DeLoach. Infant Behavior and Development, 1981, 4, 281–295.
3 *Contribution of infant characteristics to child abuse.* A.M. Frodi, Americal Journal of Mental Deficiency, 1981, 85, 4, 341–349.

5

How you can help your baby

When your baby cries, you will find doing something practical makes you feel less helpless and will often help the baby too. Your response will often involve physical contact with the baby and rhythmic activity – feeding, holding, cuddling, rocking, rubbing. The power of human touch is marvellous. It carries on throughout life, whether it means holding a crying child or rubbing a wound better.

Even as adults, when we feel upset, it often helps for someone to put their arms around us and hug us or just touch our hands. We feel security and love from the touch of another person, in the same way that babies and children do.

Breastfeeding

Breastfeeding is a very popular method of pacifying a crying baby. As one mother put it, a baby cannot scream and feed at the same time (well, not usually), and if nothing else, it gives the mother some peace. Seven of the mothers who wrote to me named breastfeeding as the most helpful way of soothing the baby.

Most unsettled babies will take a feed if offered to them, so it is often hard to know if a crying baby is hungry or just enjoys sucking for comfort. Unlike bottlefeeding, it is not thought possible to overfeed a breastfed baby, although several of my friends' crying babies grew very big very quickly through a plentiful milk supply and frequent feeding. However, in all cases the baby's weight gain slowed down after the first few months and at around the age of two, their weight was within the normal range.

A crying breastfed baby puts doubts in any mother's mind that the baby may be undernourished. Judy Dunn, a Cambridge research psychologist, found in her studies on infant crying[1] that many mothers gave up breastfeeding because they thought their supply of milk was inadequate. Confidence and flexibility were very important to successful breastfeeding. First-time mothers tended to feed on the advice of feeding schedules and their babies cried more. Mothers of second and subsequent babies would feed a crying baby any time after one and a half hours of the previous feed.

Maggie was sure that in hospital her crying baby was not hungry as she had a good supply of milk and the baby was gaining well. Maggie described her baby. 'Whether I demand fed, withheld food, expressed off first milk or gave extra water, Natalie just kept on crying all the hours she was awake, and she was awake for about 14 hours a day from birth. She was never just awake – she either was asleep or eating or awake and screaming.'

Unfortunately, breastfeeding does not ensure a contented baby, as breastfed babies are as likely to cry excessively as bottlefed babies, particularly in the evenings when they are young. Perhaps this is a reflection in part of mothers not being flexible enough in responding to the baby's hunger. There is also the problem of an abundant milk supply in the morning (sometimes too much) and a diminished supply by the late afternoon.

You may be considering giving up breastfeeding, but Jill's experience in maternity hospital is typical of mothers who give up. 'I had fully intended to breastfeed, but one night an impatient midwife snatched him off me and said "Oh, let's give him a bottle and see if that helps." This left me with a wrong impression of breastfeeding – that is, that bottlefed babies were likely to feed better and sleep more easily. In fact, it didn't help at all.' A breastfed baby may not improve on bottlefeeds. If hunger is suspected, try other measures to increase your milk supply (see the tips below). Alternatively, there may be another reason for the crying (see possible causes of babies crying on page 27) which is no more likely to improve on bottlefeeds and may in fact just get worse, for instance in the case of allergy to cow's milk.

Here are some points to consider. Breastmilk is the *perfect* food for babies. Formula bottle milk may be a substitute but it is no match for breastmilk, which contains the exact balance of all the nutrients that a baby needs at any stage in development. It contains immunities to illnesses to protect the baby for many months. Formula milks contain foreign nutrients to which babies can react or become allergic to, sometimes for a long time to come. Breastfed babies suffer from fewer infections, including gastroentiritis, which can be very serious in babies. And one advantage for you – you will get your figure back faster by breastfeeding.

More than all that, breastfeeding is a natural way of babies being fed and comforted by rhythmical sucking which helps soothe them. The closeness of the mother and baby creates a special relationship of love and dependency. There is something very satisfying about feeding your own baby with your own milk, and it is very convenient and cheap too!

Tips on breastfeeding

To help the baby and yourself with breastfeeding, here are some useful tips:

● Forget about schedules. Feed the baby on demand. This can typically be every two hours for a crying baby, perhaps even every hour in the evenings. Offer a drink of water or a dummy in between, especially if your nipples are sore, or try feeding on one side only every hour in the evening.

● Check that your let-down reflex is working properly – the tingling sensation in the breasts as the milk starts flowing.

● Do not cut down on the baby's sucking time. Let the baby decide when to finish (unless you have sore nipples, when it may be best to restrict sucking to about ten minutes on each side).

● Check the positioning of the baby on the breast, which if incorrect, can cause nipple soreness and the baby not getting enough milk at each feed. The baby's head and body should be facing your body and most of your nipple, including the areola (the darker area around it), should be inside the baby's mouth.

● If your milk supply seems to overwhelm the baby when put on the breast, express off a little of the first milk flow. Changing the position of the baby at feeding may also help (eg feed standing up or with baby's body under your arm). To reduce your overall supply of milk, try feeding on alternate breasts only at each feed for a few days.

● Check for infections, like thrush. Also check your breasts for redness, soreness or lumps, and consult your health visitor or GP if you have any problems.

● Sprays and creams sometimes help sore nipples, but often the best remedy is plain fresh air – keep your breasts bare for a while each day if it is warm enough, or just wear loose clothing. Use water and no soap to rinse your breasts. I found a cream called Kamillosan (based on chamomile) very helpful to heal cracked, sore nipples. Your chemist should stock this cream or order it for you.

● Eat a good diet. This does not mean elaborate meals. Fruit, vegetables, salads, bread, meats, fish, cheese, yoghurts, eggs – good, wholesome foods which can be thrown together for a quick nutritious meal. Current research shows that you may not need to consume extra calories, so just eat to satisfy your hunger. However, eat and drink regularly during the day and make sure you always eat breakfast and lunch. Have a drink beside you whenever you feed the baby, like water, fresh fruit juice or a herbal tea. Remember that milk, coffee, tea, cola and some squashes can upset babies, particularly in large quantities.

● Check your own diet for possible foods or drugs which are causing allergic reactions in the baby (see pages 38 to 46).

● If the baby falls asleep at the breast, put it straight down.

● At night, feed lying down on your side in bed, so that you can get back to sleep for a while.

● During the day, lie down or sit and relax whilst feeding, perhaps in the shade in the garden on a summer's day, or otherwise with your feet up, reading a book or magazine, watching television, listening to the radio or reading to a toddler. Remember that some babies prefer to concentrate on feeding without being distracted by being stroked or talked to at the same time, or having too much background noise.

● Get the evening meal ready early in the day to avoid the rush at the baby's worst time.

● Rest and relax as much as you can. One mother described the vicious circle of tiredness, tension, doing too much, reduced milk supply, baby crying, tiredness.

A frequent feeder may force you to make a decision about breastfeeding in public. It would be tragic to feel trapped inside the house all day just because the baby needs two or three hourly feeding. While breastfeeding, you can travel light, taking only spare nappies, when seeing friends or going on an outing.

I felt embarrassed to breastfeed my first baby in public, but that was nearly six years ago. When my second baby came along, I soon had enough of slipping off to the spare bedroom or the Ladies, so he was fed virtually wherever we happened to be. After all, the only time I could most sensibly join in a conversation was when the baby was quiet at the breast. It is quite possible if you wear the right clothes – like a button-down top or a baggy jumper – to feed a baby very discreetly.

It does seem a bit daft in these days of topless beaches for anyone to be prudish about a baby taking its nourishment in the way Nature intended. The more mothers breastfeed in public, the more acceptable it becomes.

Maureen Minchin gives some good advice in her books on breastfeeding and allergies.[2] She suggests that some breastfed babies could cry in the evenings because of a temporary lactose intolerance caused by too much milk in the baby's stomach from the morning feeds and this milk being pushed through to the intestines without being properly digested by the enzyme, lactase. She feels this could account for colic and gas later in the day. Her recommendation to solve this problem is to feed the baby at one breast only in the morning if the milk supply is abundant, or simply to express some milk (eg from one breast whilst feeding from the other) and keep it stored in the fridge for the evening.

Some mothers find that their breasts are so engorged (over full) with milk at night, that they wake their sleeping babies to feed them so that they feel more comfortable. Instead of waking your baby during the night, try expressing your milk and giving this extra milk to the baby after feeds in the late afternoon and evening to encourage the baby to settle down.

As with other aspects of babycare, mothers are often at the mercy of conflicting advice from family, friends and even professionals regarding breastfeeding problems. Advice can vary in hospital from midwife to midwife, and at home from health visitor to GP. Stick with one person you can trust.

Many mothers find it enormously helpful to join breastfeeding support groups, like the National Childbirth Trust, La Leche League, and the Association of Breastfeeding Mothers (addresses in Appendix 1) so that they can talk to other mothers who are breastfeeding their babies too. These groups also have trained counsellors – mothers themselves – to help with problems. Barbara had problems with breastfeeding her crying baby, but she found help at last. 'I encountered one problem after another with breastfeeding. First I had engorged breasts. This led to extreme nipple-soreness, as Steven could not "latch-on" properly. My nipples then cracked, so my midwife recommended that I wear nipple-shields. These only helped a very little. The last straw came when Steven was weighed, and I was told he was losing weight and I ought to give supplementary bottles. During this time, Steven was crying a good deal. I assumed it was from hunger. Before giving a supplementary bottle, I contacted La Leche League, as I was determined to breastfeed. They helped me to solve all my breastfeeding problems. They showed me how to position Steven on my breast so as to avoid nipple-soreness, and also told me that wearing nipple-shields can reduce the milk-supply, as there is not enough stimulation on the nipple from the baby's mouth. From then on, Steven's weight gain shot up, often to ten ounces a week.'

Finally on breastfeeding, Jane's experience should convince anyone who doubts the ability of breastmilk to sustain a baby for more than a few weeks. Jane's baby refused solids until she was eight and a half months old, but thrived happily on breastmilk alone.

Bottlefeeding

You may have already made a decision to bottlefeed your baby. For some mothers, the establishment of breastfeeding in hospital or at home proves very difficult, perhaps because they feel exhausted from the birth or encounter problems with breastfeeding, like sore nipples. Sometimes there are the added problems of a baby already crying a great deal and hardly sleeping.

Some mothers continue to breastfeed, supplementing with bottles of formula milk. However, this can be very tiring. I had difficulty fully breastfeeding my first baby, who was very sleepy at first and a difficult feeder. I was persuaded to give her supplementary bottles after two weeks as she was losing weight. She found sucking from a bottle much easier and after six weeks, there seemed little point continuing to breastfeed. I was disappointed but quite relieved in a way, as it had taken so long to feed her using both methods.

Nevertheless, it is possible to re-establish total breastfeeding and many mothers have achieved this by cutting down on the supplementary bottles or cutting them out completely and being prepared to breastfeed frequently for a while. If you want to try this, ask your health visitor or a breastfeeding counsellor for advice.

If you do regret being unable to breastfeed successfully, and some mothers do find it impossible, it is far better to accept your decision without feeling guilty and make the most of some advantages bottlefeeding brings.

Bottlefed babies can usually go longer between feeds, normally four hours, because formula milk is more concentrated than breastmilk. You will be able to leave the baby with someone else to feed whilst you get on with other chores or get out of the house for a while. You can actually see how much the baby has taken at each feed, which is reassuring for many parents.

Tips on bottlefeeding

Here are some tips which may help your crying bottlefed baby:

● Make up feeds according to the instructions on the formula tin. Do not be tempted to add more powder as this can be dangerous for the baby and can cause a condition which gives rise to the baby being irritable and fussy.

● If the baby usually vomits after the feed and fights the bottle half-way through, although appears still hungry, some professionals advise adding a bit more water to the bottle to dilute it. For instance, if you normally make up a seven ounce bottle, add seven scoops of formula powder to eight ounces of water. Sometimes, a more diluted bottle will be taken in full and not brought back. Consult your health visitor about this and keep a check of weight gain every week.

● Make sure that you clean and sterilise thoroughly bottles and other equipment. If feeds are not finished, throw the remaining milk in the bottle away.

● For convenience, make up a whole day's requirements and store it in a sterile jug or bottles in the fridge.

● Bring up the baby's wind during the feed if possible, perhaps halfway, as well as afterwards.

● Do not forget that bottlefed babies may need drinks of water or juice in between feeds, particularly in warm weather.

● You can try different types of bottles and teats but many parents find the expense and trouble of experimenting with alternatives makes little difference. I found that the Playtex bottles with collapsable inner bags seemed to reduce the baby's intake of air a little.

● Check that the hole in the teat is the right size. Hold the bottle upside down over the sink to ensure the correct flow of milk which should be a steady drip.

● Test the milk's temperature by dropping a little milk on to the back of your hand. It should feel warm and *not* hot.

● Bottled water, as an alternative to tap water, to make up feeds may be worth a try if all else has failed (Malvern water or Highland Spring water are recommended). If it helps, buy a water filter to use (see page 43). If there is no improvement after two weeks, return to tap water for the sake of convenience.

● Consult your GP about the possibility of allergy to the formula used.

● Even though you may be exhausted or want to get on with something else, never leave the bottle propped in the baby's mouth, as some babies have gagged and choked from this in the past.

● Microwave ovens are not recommended to heat up bottles. There have been some recent cases of babies' mouths and throats being seriously scalded from drinks heated in microwaves. This is because the container may stay cool whilst the contents can be hot. If you must use a microwave make sure that you shake the bottle to distribute the contents evenly and then test the temperature of the fluid on the back of your hand every time.

Like my baby daughter, bottlefed babies can be difficult feeders, no matter what you try to do to help. One mother described the problems she had feeding her baby. 'To get her to drink anything, we had to try to fool her in any way possible. Dip her dummy in gripewater, although at the beginning I was going to do everything right, then her teat in the same, swap them quickly and she may take another ounce. Or rock her for ages until she stopped crying, pop in the bottle when eyes were closed – she may take an ounce.'

Seventeen mothers who wrote to me said their babies were bottlefed from birth. A further 13 babies were bottlefed after a few weeks of breastfeeding; unfortunately, for nearly all the babies there was no immediate improvement, except one. Pauline wrote about transferring from breast to bottle which she did due to her more than ample supply of milk. At eight weeks, she decided to wean her baby on to SMA formula milk, against medical advice. 'This I did and never had any further problems. My two successive children were fed solely on SMA.'

Non-nutritive sucking

All babies derive comfort from sucking, as well as food, and it actually relaxes the baby's muscles and stomach. Sucking can be on the breast, bottle or a dummy, or it may be on the baby's own fingers, thumb or fist. Crying babies often have trouble soothing themselves in this way. Try and help the baby find fingers or thumb by leaving hands uncovered and available to put in the baby's mouth.

Dummies, or pacifiers, are excellent ways of soothing a fretful baby – I would never have survived my two babies without a dummy. Some babies do not take to them readily, but it is worth persevering. A dummy helped ten of the babies whose mothers wrote to me. Two of them continued having a dummy for longer than their mothers would have liked. If you want to wean your baby off a dummy, choose the three to four months period. However, my children continued to have a dummy to fall asleep with for three years and it never bothered any of us. Premature babies have even been found to develop quicker when regularly given a dummy.

Make sure the dummies you use conform to BSI standard and buy new ones regularly. Keep them clean by sterilising them in between use. Keep a couple of spares in the steriliser.

Christine has this advice about dummies. 'If anyone tells you that dummies are dreadful dirty things and never to use one, ignore them. Amy's dummy proved to be a great comfort to her (and us). I never said "my child won't have a dummy" and even bought one beforehand! You can regulate when they have a dummy, unlike a thumb. Amy still has her dummy at bedtime and finds a lot of comfort in it.'

Parents of fretful babies are sometimes tempted or advised to dip dummies in sugar or honey, or to give sweet drinks from bottles or dinky feeders. However, the alarming evidence is that long term use can rot teeth even before they are properly grown. In the long run, feeder cups are better than bottles but sugary drinks should be avoided. Dummies without sugar or honey are unlikely to do any harm.

Wind or tummy pain

There is some controversy between childcare experts as to whether babies experience pain because of the gas or wind that accumulates in their intestines. The experience of many parents is that babies, particularly colicky ones, do seem to be troubled by the passage of gas which can often be heard rumbling around the digestive system. Once the wind is passed, either up or down, temporary relief is often provided. For some babies, a small amount of milk is regularly brought back with each burp. There is nothing to worry about this, unless the vomit changes colour or is violently expelled.

Colicky babies often have distended or hard stomachs during colic attacks which seem to indicate that air is trapped in the baby's guts. The reason for this may be due to the way the baby sucks on the breast or bottle – some babies take in more air when feeding than others. A poor breastmilk supply can cause more air to be sucked in as the baby struggles to obtain the milk. An excessive milk supply can cause the baby to gulp in air with milk. Sucking on an empty bottle or a bottle which is not tilted up far enough to fill the teat with milk, will cause air to be taken into the tummy. Crying spells can also account for air being taken in gasps. Some babies may be producing gas in their intestines as part of an allergic reaction.

If your baby suffers from excessive wind, try holding the baby in a more upright position during feeding. Try and bring up some wind during the feed, as well as afterwards, by holding the baby upright or leaning slightly forward on your lap whilst you gently rub the baby's back. It is not usually worth spending more than a few minutes trying to bring up a burp. Other favourite positions to hold a windy baby are upright against your left shoulder, facing outwards upright on your hip, or face down across your lap. A warm bottle wrapped in a towel for the baby to lie on may bring some relief. Try massaging the baby on just the tummy with warmed oil (see the section on baby massage on page 69). Bending the baby's legs gently towards the tummy and out straight again might also help relieve wind.

Another useful tip is to raise the level of the head end of the pram, cot or crib by placing a flattish pillow under the mattress. Colicky babies usually prefer sleeping on their tummies.

Some gripewater before feeds can help, or some warmed boiled water may work. Sedatives before feeds might help in severe cases of colic, so ask your GP for advice. See also section on herbal remedies, page 73.

Eileen's baby was still suffering from excessive wind at the time of writing. She says 'Grace is nine months old now and from three weeks old, myself or my husband have not had one complete night sleep. The only sleep we get is if my husband takes her one night and I take her the next. During the night we rub her back and change her from side to side, to disturb the wind, or she might release it. Then she can get another hour sleep.'

Comfort by movement

As all parents know, babies derive great comfort from movement, perhaps reminding them of the motion they experienced in the mother's uterus.

In the survey published by *Parents* magazine, nine out of ten mothers cuddled and rocked their crying babies. Nine of the 63 babies in my survey were comforted by movement, eg car rides, pram rides or a sling.

In traditional cultures, the young are often carried in slings and excessive crying is rare. You can also use a sling to carry your baby around. Alison found that the best thing she did to help ease her baby's crying, was to buy a sling. 'If Laura wasn't at the breast, she was strapped to my chest, thus enabling me to perform some housework and simple cooking.' Juliet also found that 'Walking the baby around the block in the sling was one solution.' Parents in a

Swedish maternity hospital were given a baby carrier to take home and at a three month follow-up the majority reported great success at stopping the baby crying.

Other common ways of keeping a baby on the move are prams, rocking cradles, rocking chairs, swings and baby bouncers for older babies (harnesses which suspend from the ceiling). Several companies have recently marketed some new ideas to help maintain movement without too much effort, eg bouncing cradles and pram rockers.[3]

Pram rides and car rides have proved time-honoured ways of getting a baby to sleep. One mother who wrote to me resorted to car rides at night but she continued 'It got to be a habit. We'd be out until three or four in the morning just to get her to sleep. Sometimes, she'd wake up when we pulled up outside our house and start all over again.'

You will probably try many of these methods of soothing your baby, but very often, parents carry and walk about with their babies in their arms, rocking, patting, rubbing their backs, singing or hushing them with words of comfort.

Research studies looked at the optimum rocking rate to calm a crying baby and they found it to be quite fast, at 60 to 90 rocks per minute.[4] These studies also showed that *intermittent vertical* rocking (up and down) was more successful in bringing a baby to a calm alert state, whereas *continuous horizontal* rocking (to and fro) was more likely to promote sleep.

Comfort by sound

Another popular method of soothing a crying baby is by sound. A newborn baby quickly recognises and responds to its mother's voice, so talk and sing to your baby (no guarantee that shouting works!). Lullabies seem to have evolved especially to calm babies with their repetitive, monotonous melodies. You can make a tape recording of yourself singing, if it helps. Musical boxes or mobiles playing a tune over and over can also help. Turn the music on every time you put the baby down to sleep. I found it seemed to condition my two babies to sleep and they would start going drowsy after a few turns of Brahms Lullaby.

In fact, it seems that any repetitive noise, which is loud and continuous, may work. Christine found her baby was soothed by the noises of the hairdryer and hoover. She says: 'Eventually, I tape recorded my hoover on a half hour tape and I would play it to her whilst I left the room.'

Babies can even be calmed by the sound of a baby crying – including their own crying. Even if a tape recording were to be effective, it would seem to defeat the object of the exercise for the parents.

A very useful investment to comfort the baby would be a baby soothing cassette (known as 'womb music'), which mimics the sounds heard in the uterus. The noise of a radio band off the air might do just as well. The tapes are available by mail order[5] and should be introduced during the first ten weeks of life for maximum effectiveness. Three mothers who wrote to me reported great success with these tapes. I too went into hospital to have my second baby armed with a cassette of womb music (just in case . . .) and it worked very well most of the time. Many is the night at home that the baby, my husband and I eventually fell asleep to that whirring noise.

A nursing officer at a Sheffield maternity hospital compared the effectiveness of womb music to musical boxes and other calming methods used by mothers.[6] The cassette of womb sounds was by far the most successful method of calming a fretful baby, with a 98% success rate.

Sally described how sound helped her and her baby. 'When Katie was a few months old and we couldn't shut her up we used to put on a tape of Incantation – South American music. I would dance around the room with her. It nearly always stopped her and sent her to sleep sometimes.'

Comfort by light

Some babies seem to sleep better with a soft, perhaps pink, light in their bedroom. Others prefer a completely dark room. It is a good idea to let babies sleep in natural light during the day (in the open air or by a window) to encourage them to distinguish between day and night.

Comfort by swaddling

The practice of swaddling has dwindled in our society but is still popular in some other societies, where babies may even be strapped to a cradle board too.

It may go against your better judgement to restrict a baby's movements in this way, but child development specialists believe that swaddling is effective in calming babies because it reduces the amount of stimulation the baby experiences from the involuntary movements of its arms and legs.

Probably a good compromise is to wrap the baby firmly, but not too tightly, in a blanket or a cotton sheet in summer, tucking in arms. If in doubt, a midwife or a health visitor will show you how to do this. If the baby can suck a thumb or fingers, leave one hand out when you put the baby down to sleep.

If your baby is a difficult feeder, it might help to swaddle the baby as described during feeding.

Comfort by touch

Parents naturally rub and stroke their fretful babies to calm them. In some countries, like India, it is common practice to massage babies with warmed natural plant oils. It helps to protect the baby's skin from the hot sun, but it also helps soothe and relax babies. It has the added advantage of promoting closeness and mutual confidence between mother and baby.

In her book, the Baby Massage Book,[7] Tina Heinl describes how massage helped her babies. She suggests that you set aside 20 minutes each morning to sit in a quiet warm room or outside in warm weather, take the baby's clothes off and put an old towel over your lap. Place the baby on your lap and massage the baby all over with hand-warm oil. Coconut oil is recommended, but any vegetable or baby oil would do,

Follow the massage with a bath for the baby, or maybe for both of you. It does not matter if the oil is washed off afterwards. After this, the baby should fall into a deep relaxed sleep. Some babies do not respond to massage well at first and may cry, but if you persevere, most babies come to love it. And it is very helpful for relaxing colicky babies.

Another method of helping by touch is stroking. If your baby is extra sensitive, this method might work well. It involves gently holding the baby's head with both hands for a few minutes at start and finish. In between, the baby's body is gently and lightly stroked in downward movements which are each repeated three times. The whole exercise lasts about 15 minutes. Developed by a doctor at a London hospital,[8] this technique of stroking has greatly helped the development and temperament of premature babies, for whom massage would be too vigorous. The babies who were stroked were more alert and even developed faster mentally.

Low birth weight babies have also gained weight faster and benefited from being nursed on a sheepskin (otherwise known as a lambskin or fleecy blanket).[9] Susan's first baby was a crier, but she writes 'For my latest baby, I bought him a sheepskin to sleep on and he likes to cuddle into that.' Babies can lie straight on to them, preferably on their tummies, to gain full benefit of the comfort from the texture. Sometimes, the baby reacts to the wool by a rash, but if this is the case, try covering the sheepskin with a cotton sheet.

Bath the baby

Bathing can help calm a fussy baby. Baths together can be fun and increase the opportunity for physical contact as well as giving the baby added security in water. Baths are traditionally given to babies in the morning, but a baby can be bathed any time of the day or evening, if it helps. If a baby really hates being bathed, topping and tailing is quite adequate.

A few babies hate being pulled about being dressed and undressed, in which case keep clothing easy (e.g. babygrows). There is no need to change the baby's clothes at night – just change them when they get dirty.

Play with the baby

Talking and playing with the baby provide a distraction from discomfort and misery. Take it gently at first to see how much the baby tolerates. Start off by showing the baby interesting objects or toys, then let the baby touch and hold them. Any safe household object will be of interest. An older baby will examine the object by putting it in its mouth too.

Strap colourful mobiles or rattles across the pram or the cot. Watching other children play or adults working can be an excellent pastime. Frequently change the baby's perspective. A reclining baby chair is an ideal way of the baby seeing all around, and you can bounce it with one foot while cooking! Do not balance the chair on a worktop or table as it could overbalance as the baby bounces.

Let the baby kick on a blanket on the floor, perhaps in the warm sunshine by a window. Alison's baby liked to kick with no nappy on. She describes 'Many evenings were passed, watching Laura lying on her changing mat. It did at least ease her crying.'

Some babies enjoy more energetic exercise and play and a book called Baby Gymnastics[10] will give you some ideas.

It can be a shock to realise that your baby is very wakeful, so try play and social contact instead of spending many frustrating hours trying to get the baby off to sleep. Hand the baby over to play with dad too.

Help with discomfort

A baby who is uncomfortable or in pain is likely to cry more and sleep less.

Teething, although often blamed for all sorts of evils, does seem to bother many babies. Teeth start being cut during the early months (some babies are even born teething) and during this time, gums can be sore and swollen, and cheeks and ears are often red. Excessive dribbling and compulsive biting on objects usually herald the emergence of a tooth. There are gels available which may help, as do teething rings kept cool in the fridge. Homoeopathic teething granules might also help. Paracetamol may be necessary when teething is particularly painful – check with your GP or health visitor about this.

Being too hot or too cold will also produce discomfort and distress. It is more likely that a baby is over- rather than under-dressed, and overheating a baby can be dangerous. An overheated baby will be sweaty and flushed. Feel the back of the baby's neck. If it is sweaty, the baby may be too hot. I always used to go by what I felt comfortable wearing and added one extra layer for the baby. Just one or two blankets over the baby's babygrow or clothes should be ample whilst the baby sleeps, even in winter if the house is well heated. Remember to give the baby drinks in hot weather as well as feeds.

If your baby is cold, a sheepskin may help to keep the pram or cot cosy. You can warm the cot first with a warm water botle and remove it when you put the baby down. Sleepsuits are helpful for a baby who kicks off covers.

Clothing which is uncomfortable may cause redness or rashes and irritability. Common problem areas are around the nappy where plastic pants often cause irritation to the skin. Try using a larger size of pants or if you use disposable nappies, try leaving off plastic pants altogether.

Biological washing powders and fabric conditioner can cause irritation to the skin. Try using soap flakes to wash the baby's clothes and bed linen. Some fabrics cause reactions too – smooth cotton or pure wool are least likely to cause problems. Beware using nylon wool in knitted mittens and booties as the threads have been known to wind around fingers and toes and harm them.

Nappy rash is experienced at some time by most babies. It is uncomfortable for the baby and may lead to infection. To prevent nappy rash, change the baby frequently and give the baby a while each day to lie without a nappy, so that the baby's bottom is exposed to fresh air. Cleanse the nappy area thoroughly at each nappy change, preferably with water and mild baby soap. Baby wipes can irritate the skin. Dry the skin completely and use a barrier cream, like zinc and castor oil. If the nappy area develops a rash or becomes sore, ask the health visitor for advice on appropriate treatment.

If you use terry towelling nappies, a one-way nappy liner may help prevent nappy rash. It is important that the nappies are soaked in a sterilising solution which is changed daily, and then thoroughly washed and rinsed. Drying them on the line will help get rid of bacteria and keep them white. Iron the nappies to make them soft again.

Disposable nappies are very convenient and not now regarded as an expensive luxury. They can be bought in bulk from supermarkets and even delivered by some chainstores, eg Mothercare. However, some babies' skin reacts to the fabric of the nappies – try different brands. Plastic pants over disposable nappies, particularly if tight, are likely to cause soreness and nappy rash as moisture cannot evaporate away.

Anything else?

Gripewater and colic drops may help a crying baby, but I never found them to be at all effective with my babies. Do not give the baby any alcohol, although older relatives may suggest it. You can easily give an overdose, which could be fatal for a baby or small child, particularly on an empty stomach.

Homoeopathy was recommended by Hazel, a midwife, who wrote to me. She related the experience of a friend who had a crying third baby. After six months of grizzling her friend took the baby to a homoeopath who prescribed a remedy which worked within hours. Carol also wrote about how a homoeopath helped her own depression and also helped settle her child's erratic behaviour and continued tantrums. It is advisable to consult a homoeopath rather than buying remedies over the counter. The British Homoeopathic Association will recommend a doctor practising homoepathy in your area (see Appendix 1 for address).

Herbal remedies have been used for countless years to help babies. Jane, who runs a La Leche League support group, wrote about one mother's solution to crying – an Indian remedy for colic, where the breastfeeding mother takes fennel tea or chews the seeds. Another mother in Jane's group had been advised by a herbalist to take strong chamomile tea herself for a sleepless baby.

Babies can be given direct an infusion of crushed dill seeds to relieve colic. In Barbara Griggs' book 'The Home Herbal',[11] she describes how to make the infusion. 'Put a couple of teaspoons of dill seeds in a jug, pour half a pint of boiling water over them, and let them steep, covered, for 10 minutes. Cool and strain.' Give a teaspoon to the baby from time to time during colic bouts. Infusions of fennel seeds or caraway seeds can be similarly used for colic, made in the same way. A manufactured fennel baby drink is now available although the sugar content is quite high.

A few teaspoons of warm chamomile tea is particularly recommended for sleeplessness in babies and small children. Chamomile tea can be bought in tea bags from most health shops and supermarkets. Catnip tea, lemon balm or lemon verbena infusions can also be used for sleeplessness. Chamomile and catnip teas are also recommended for mild cases of diarrhoea in babies.

Cranial osteopathy helped two of the crying babies amongst my letters. The treatment involves a careful examination of the baby, seeking indications of injury or malfunction which might have been present since birth or soon after. The corrective manual treatment, which should be carried out only by a registered osteopath, is so gentle it can be used safely on any baby from birth onwards. The General Council and Register of Osteopaths will supply names of registered osteopaths in your area (see Appendix 1 for address).

Amanda wrote about her baby who at 11 months was still screaming and had temper tantrums. They were both admitted for three days to the baby unit of the local hospital but the baby was no better. The next day in desperation, Amanda sought the advice of an osteopath who suggested cranial osteopathy. "We haven't looked back since. She changed overnight. She occasionally has to have top up treatment. When we moved recently she didn't sleep for a month. I took her for a treatment and she has slept ever since.'

Elaine also wrote about her fourth baby who cried a great deal. Her doctor told her it was colic and that she just had to put up with it. However, she continues 'My aunt who is an osteopath came to see us a couple of days later and said she would check Guy over for me. She found he had a muscle out of place in his neck which she put back in place. It was like magic – he became a normal baby overnight and actually slept for six hours that night!'

Combination of responses

One study showed how a combination of responses – sound, light, temperature and swaddling – was found most effective in promoting sleep and decreasing crying in babies.[12] Swaddling was the most effective single method of helping the baby. So using a few different methods at the same time may help your baby best.

I used to find I could settle my baby son best by rocking the pram, whilst he sucked on his dummy and listened to a baby soothing cassette. However, some babies who are very sensitive may be overwhelmed by too many responses, so if your baby is easily startled and responds better to a quiet life, try one thing at a time and take the pace slowly (see section on babies with low sensory threshold on page 34).

Babies have different 'states' of arousal: sleep, a quiet alert state, a crying state, and transitional states when they are changing from one state to another. Difficult babies often have trouble controlling their state and flip into the crying state very easily. The comforting techniques described in this Chapter will help your baby regain control. Remember that in order to interact with your baby, it is important to bring the baby to a quiet alert state if possible.

Some of the ways of helping the baby may not work well for your baby, others may work at times, and others are almost guaranteed to work for a while. June found a number of things helped. They included a dummy and gripewater, which sometimes soothed the baby for a little while, but usually for only five or ten minutes. She also found a baby-sling was useful. The baby would be okay for maybe 30 minutes in that. However, the only time the baby was really quiet was when she was at the breast, therefore June was feeding more or less constantly.

It is important for you to have a few options open so that you do not feel helpless if one thing does not work. The checklist on page 76 gives a number of alternatives you can try to help the baby.

Be guided by what the baby responds well to and be prepared to be flexible. What works in one situation may not work well in another. What works at one age may not work a few weeks later. It is easy to get stuck on one response too, every time the baby cries, although it may not always be the appropriate one (like always feeding or always using a dummy). On the other hand, do not rush from one thing to another, not giving enough time for anything to work.

Observe how the baby reacts in different situations (eg out in the pram, having a bath, feeding) at different times of the day or with different people. Watch too for the way the baby develops and

Checklist on how to help the baby

Baby hungry?
Breastfeed or bottlefeed.

Baby thirsty?
Offer drink: spoon or bottle.

Baby in pain?
Offer dummy, breast, bottle.

Give warmed boiled water, gripe-water, herbal remedy.

Massage baby or just tummy.

Hold baby, cuddle, walk about.

Change position of baby (upright, facing down across your lap).

Rock baby up and down.

Use sling.

Consult health visitor or GP.

Baby tired but fights sleep?
Offer dummy, breast, bottle.

Rock horizontally in your arms or in pram.

Try a pram rocker, rocking cradle or bouncing cradle.

Change position of cot or pram.

Quieter or noisier environment.

Leave to cry for short while.

Check lighting: softer light, darker room.

Use baby soother cassette, sing to baby, musical box.

Try rhythmic noises eg clock ticking, hoover, hairdryer.

Try pram instead of cot, or cot instead of pram.

Baby too cold? Too warm?

Use fleecy blanket (sheepskin).

Car rides or walks with pram.

Let baby sleep in fresh air.

Try baby massage and warm bath.

Try swaddling.

Check for illness or allergies with your GP or health visitor.

Baby fighting at the breast?
Check baby's position at the breast (body and head should be facing you).

Check that most of your nipple is inside baby's mouth.

Check nose free of breast (head should be tilted back slightly).

Let baby suck on dummy and substitute breast quickly.

Cold and blocked nose? Consult health visitor or GP.

Check let-down reflex working – the tingling sensation in breasts as milk starts flowing.

Check breasts for soreness.

Change feeding position eg standing up, lying down.

Too much milk? Express some off before feeds, or feed on one breast, changing sides at each feed, for a few days.

Too little milk? Feed more frequently. Save expressed breast-milk and give after feeds.

Consult health visitor or GP, or a breastfeeding counsellor.

Checklist on how to help the baby – *continued*

Difficulty bottlefeeding?

Try different bottle or teat.

Check hole in teat not too big or small.

Offer bottles more frequently for a few days.

Try warmed boiled water before feed or a herbal remedy.

Leave for half an hour and try feeding again.

Check for allergies.

Consult health visitor or GP.

Baby uncomfortable?

Change nappy.

Try different nappies or leave off plastic pants.

Let baby kick with no nappy on.

Check for nappy rash – consult health visitor or GP.

Check for clothing rashes.

Baby too hot? Remove some clothing and offer drinks.

Baby too cold? Add clothing, including mittens, booties, hat.

Try fleecy blanket (sheepskin)

Extra sensitive baby?

Quiet environment.

Keep to routine and limit visitors.

Do not overwhelm baby with stimulation, particularly when feeding.

Handle and talk to baby gently.

Swaddle baby.

Stroke baby, using stroking technique (not whilst feeding).

Baby generally cranky?

Talk to baby.

Play with baby; use toys or safe household objects.

Let baby kick on floor with no nappy on.

Use sling.

Use bouncing chair or baby bouncer.

Take baby out in pram or buggy.

Visit a friend.

Comfort by sucking, rocking, movement, noise, swaddling.

Feed baby.

Massage baby and give warm bath.

Check for illness, infection, diarrhoea, allergies.

Consult health visitor or GP.
Consult homoeopath, cranial osteopath, try herbal remedies.

Still crying?

Put the baby down and walk out of room.

Give baby to someone else if possible.

Go out with baby.

Phone your health visitor, GP, CRY-SIS contact, friend, relative.

changes. For instance, the baby's reactions to strangers will change as the baby gets older, and the baby will start becoming upset if the mother looks seriously or unsmiling at her baby.

Sometimes, on hitting upon something which works well, you inadvertently establish a habit, like rocking the baby to sleep, which at a later stage you will want to break. The long-term objective should be to gradually reduce your involvement in calming the baby or inducing sleep.

Notes

1 *Distress and comfort*, Judy Dunn. Fontana, 1977.
2 *Breastfeeding matters*, Maureen Minchin. Alma Publications and George Allen and Unwin, 1985. *Food for thought*, Maureen Minchin. Oxford University Press, 1986.
3 The Lullababy Vertical Rocker and the Minder Automatic Pram Rocker are examples of these – addresses in Appendix 1.
4 *The soothing effects of rocking as determined by the direction and frequency of movement*, D.R. Pederson. Canadian Journal of Behavioural Science, 1975, 7, 237–243. *Rocking as a soothing intervention: The influence of direction and type of movement*, J.M. Byrne and F.D. Horowitz. Infant Behaviour and Development, 1981, 4, 207–218.
5 Jaygee Cassettes and Lullababy produce tapes of womb sounds. See Appendix 1 for addresses.
6 *The testing and comparision of the intra-uterine sound against other methods for calming babies*, P.M. Callis. Midwives Chronicle, October 1984, 336–338.
7 *The baby massage book*, Tina Heinl. Conventure Ltd., 1982.
8 Dr. Didi Adamson-Macedo currently works in the Special Care Baby unit at St. George's hospital, South London. *The tender touch* article in Parents Magazine, November 1985, featured her technique.
9 These blankets can be bought at some baby specialist shops or direct from the manufacturer Winganna (see Appendix 1 for address).
10 *Baby gymnastics*. A. Balaskas and P. Walker. Unwin, 1985.
11 *The home herbal*. Barbara Griggs. Pan, 1983.
12 *Cumulative effects of continuous stimulation on arousal level in infants*, Y. Brackbill. Child Development, 1971, 42. 17–26.

6

How to survive the nights

It is one thing when a baby cries all day – it is quite another when a baby cries at night.

During the first few weeks of life, most babies start sleeping less in the day and more at night. The typical age for a baby to sleep a five-hour stretch at night is three months. For the majority of parents, getting up to feed or otherwise see to a baby several times each night is part of life during the early months.

Continued sleep problems, like difficulty settling and night waking, are very common in older babies and toddlers. About a third of children are still waking regularly during the night at the age of one. These problems are discussed on page 124, but this section is really aimed at babies under six months.

People describe 'good' babies as ones who sleep well at night. This implies that wakeful babies or light sleepers are 'bad' babies and being naughty. In fact, there are many factors which affect the baby's ability to sleep soundly at night; for instance birth difficulties have been linked to frequent night waking.[1]

Undoubtedly, during the early months babies wake through hunger, thirst or discomfort. They may also be aware of their parents' absence during periods of light sleep, and be unable to settle themselves back to sleep.

Most mothers breastfeed or bottlefeed their awakened babies, which is often successful in quietening a baby and usually promotes a further period of sleep.

You might think that the introduction of solid food during the day would encourage a baby to sleep longer at night, but this does not seem to be true. However, it is a good idea to ensure that you are breastfeeding frequently enough during the day. Squeezing several feeds in during the evening may help a breastfed baby to sleep longer at night.

How to help your baby at night

Should you respond quickly to your crying baby at night, or not? For most parents, this decision is already made for them because they wake up instantly the baby starts crying and no matter how tired they feel, lying in bed listening to a moaning baby is like a form of torture. Then, of course, most families have neighbours who they fear will also be woken by the baby's crying. A few babies might well settle back to sleep if left for a few minutes, but if hunger or discomfort have caused the break of sleep, it will be a long time before the baby will cry itself back to sleep, and it would almost certainly be quicker and easier on your nerves to get up to the baby.

There are a few ways you can try to encourage your baby to sleep better at night.

You can help your baby learn the difference between night and day. During the day, the baby can sleep in a pram in the open air or by a window. Surprisingly, most babies will take naps in the midst of the family activities and it may indeed help to reinstate the difference between days, which are bright, interesting and noisy, and nights, which are dark, boring and quiet (you hope).

Any noise which comes and goes, like a central heating boiler going on and off, may cause the baby to waken. However, a continuous rhythmical noise might keep the baby asleep longer, for instance a clock ticking. Jane hit on the idea of buying an aquarium for her baby's bedroom and immediately the baby slept better at night because of the sound of the motor vibrating and the soft light.

Baby soothing cassettes of womb music may also help settle a baby back to sleep. Dummies and security objects, like a blanket or a favourite teddy which the baby strokes or sucks, often promote sleep. If your baby has not become attached to any special object, try introducing a suitable soft toy every time you put the baby down for a sleep. Swaddling may help too (see page 69).

There is no need to change a baby's nappy at night unless the baby passes a bowel movement or seems particularly bothered. Use a double terry nappy or a nappy pad inside a disposable nappy to absorb the extra moisture. Check that the baby is not too hot or too cold during the night.

When you feed the baby at night, do this with as little fuss and stimulation as possible. Taking the baby back to your bed, with maybe just a light shining through from the landing or hall, is an ideal way of keeping you both warm and sleepy.

On the other hand, here is an unusual idea to get babies to sleep longer at night, devised by some American researchers[2]: you actually *wake* the baby up 15 minutes before the normal time the baby wakes for a feed. (This may not be at a regular hour of course, but some babies do seem to always wake at around a certain time of the night). You feed the baby and make it a nice time, by playing a musical box and giving the baby cuddles. The next night, you wake the baby again, but this time, 15 – 30 minutes later than the night before. You continue waking the baby for a feed, later and later each night, until you have achieved a reasonably long stretch of sleep. The researchers found that it worked!

How to settle the baby

Once your baby is about three months old you should start establishing a regular routine in the evenings to settle the baby for the night. This may have to start quite late in the evening if your baby is still unsettled at that time of day, but it is still worth doing.

The settling routine is a way of winding the baby down from daytime activities and preparing for a quieter period at night. It could include a bath, dressing into night clothes, a breastfeed/bottlefeed, a song or quiet play in the bedroom and then put the baby down, with a dummy or comfort object, and leave the bedroom. This is not the time for boisterous play, so be warned of fathers who come home just at the time the baby is being settled for the night and want a good romp! It is, however, a good idea for the baby to get used to being settled by both parents, if possible.

Your aim with the settling routine is to help the baby settle on its own. A baby who falls asleep on the breast or bottle will miss the nipple or teat immediately on waking during the night. If your baby does fall asleep during feeding in the evening, try bringing the feed forward a half an hour, so that the baby is not exhausted by the time you offer a feed.

Babies develop a number of sometimes odd ways of settling themselves to sleep – sucking thumbs or fingers, sucking dummies, fondling security objects, stroking blankets, twiddling ears, rocking themselves or even banging their heads against the cot. Some babies only seem to fall asleep after a good few minutes crying.

If the baby cries once you have left the room, go back five or 10 minutes later, but try not to pick the baby up. Just settle the baby again quickly and leave.

Once you have established an acceptable routine, you can start bringing it forward by 15 minutes each evening until it is at a time which seems to suit the baby – probably between 6 and 8 p.m. by about five or six months of age. Some babies may seem ready to settle early in the evening and will sleep soundly until the early hours of the morning. If this is the case, see it as a good sign that the baby has started to take a long sleep during the night, albeit not at the time you would like. Lifting and feeding the baby as you go to bed often helps the baby sleep longer. Some parents go to bed early themselves to take advantage of this quiet time.

Try and make sure that the days are full of interesting activities and plenty of fresh air if possible, although over-excitement in the late afternoon and evening can cause sleeping difficulty at night. Babies do not necessarily sleep better by cutting out daytime naps, so try and ensure that your baby has at least one or two sleeps during the day.

Single parents might not wish to encourage a settling routine, keeping the baby up for company. But later on, this can cause problems if the parent wants to go out in the evening.

Where the baby sleeps

Some parents find a baby sleeps better in a pram rather than a cot or crib, or vice versa. Ann wrote about her baby. 'By five months he had outgrown his pram. We bought him a pushchair then. For his morning and afternoon sleeps, I put him in his cot with his musical mobile. He would cry for about 10 minutes, then sleep. Now he sleeps in the cot in the afternoons and doesn't cry. He cuddles his teddy, has a little sing, then goes to sleep. Obviously he didn't like his pram but felt quite content in his cot.'

You could try turning the cot, crib or pram around to another direction, i.e. from north/south to east/west, or the other way round. It sometimes works and well worth a try. A baby might wake during the night if the cot or crib is positioned against an outside wall, which will often be the coldest part of the room.

Many parents have the baby's pram or cot in their own bedroom at night, perhaps next to their bed, either for their own convenience or because the baby sleeps more soundly.

On the other hand, some babies are disturbed by your own tossing and turning or snoring during the night and sleep better in their own room. Sometimes, an older baby will surprisingly sleep better in the same bedroom as a brother or sister.

Try putting one of your well-worn, unwashed garments in the baby's cot or pram at night. Sometimes, your 'smell' will keep the baby asleep longer.

In many traditional societies throughout the world, babies sleep with their parents at night, often until a few years of age. Even in England, this was quite usual until around the 18th Century, when new ideas about hygiene and prudery became popular. In our modern day society, more and more parents find that sharing their bed with their baby works for them when all else fails. The theory that parents may suffocate a baby whilst asleep has not been proved. In fact, it seems from observations of a family asleep, that parents instinctively keep clear of the baby. The only danger is when parents are heavily sedated with alcohol or drugs.

Some parents who share their bed with the baby find it more reassuring to push the bed against the wall or to put the mattress on the floor, or even put two mattresses together to give you all more room. It is also wise to keep the baby's clothing at night light to avoid overheating in the warmth of the family bed.

I used to regularly nod off with my baby sucking at the breast in bed, but my husband and I found it uncomfortable sleeping for long with the baby in our bed, so it was not a solution for us. Nevertheless, it has worked for some of my friends who feel that the advantages – a better night's sleep – far outway the disadvantages. Potentially, a baby may expect to stay with the parents for many months to come, but with careful management it is quite possible to move the baby into its own cot, particularly once a better pattern of sleeping is established.

Sleeplessness and allergies

An allergy or sensitivity to a food or drink may be causing your baby's sleeplessness, so think hard about this possibility. Consult your health visitor or GP too for advice.

Allergies are discussed in detail on page 38. The most common culprits to cause sleeplessness are cow's milk and food additives, like the yellow orange artificial colouring, tartrazine (E102). Children affected by these substances are more likely to be unusually thirsty, so when they wake up, they will gladly take a drink or bottle – often of the very substance to which they are reacting, eg cow's milk, squash or fresh orange juice. June had three children who all reacted to cow's milk and settled to better sleeping once they were put on goat's milk at an older age.

Several parents I have spoken to have found that their children have a tolerance level of cow's milk or fruit juices. For instance, if the child has cow's milk after lunchtime, he or she might wake up several times during the night. Sometimes, just cutting out the evening bottle of milk has done the trick. Sleeplessness can also coincide with the introduction of a food like wheat or eggs.

Although sedatives may help break a pattern of frequent waking, sometimes they only make matters worse or only work for a short time. (See section on drugs and sedatives for the baby, page 120).

How to get through the night

Try and accept night waking and think of it as a temporary period. Try all the tips mentioned and don't give up hope. You and your baby will get there in the end. It can be very disheartening especially if a baby settles down to sleep well at night and after a while, regresses back to waking frequently. This may be because of illness or teething, or just because the baby is going through a particularly insecure stage. If you are concerned about your baby's sleeping pattern, consult your health visitor or GP. Talk too with other parents to find out how common night waking is; although you feel you must be the only person in the whole town who is up during the awful twilight zone of 3 a.m., you will soon discover that you are not.

Share the responsibility of getting up for the baby with your partner, if possible. Make the most of this advantage if you are bottlefeeding. Even if you are breastfeeding, it is possible to express enough milk over the course of a few days (it keeps in the fridge for 24 hours or can be frozen) for someone else to take over for one blissful night.

If you have difficulty getting back to sleep once awake during the night, try relaxation (see page 96), read a light book or magazine, listen to the radio, or if you are lucky enough to have a video recorder, watch something missed from the day before. Try and take your mind off the baby, so that you are not lying in bed waiting for the baby to wake up again. Try eating, or take a milky drink, or a herbal tea. And get yourself a nice hot water bottle – you will get very cold wandering around the house at night.

Anne's remarks may give you some encouragement for a better future. 'I never thought I would see the day when my son would sleep at night. Now, I can turn on the lights and do a war-dance in this bedroom – he never wakes up!'

Notes
1 *Why some babies don't sleep.* M. Richards and J. Bernal. New Society, 28th February 1974.
2 *In search of the sandman: shaping an infant to sleep.* R.J. McGarr and M.F. Hovell, Education and Treatment of Children, 1980, 3, 173–182.

7

How you can help yourself

This Chapter is written mainly with mothers in mind but much of it will apply to fathers as well. The first important step to helping yourself is to realise that having a crying, sleepless baby makes tremendous demands on you. Then you have to meet the needs of any other children, your partner, the home, yourself and possibly other members of your family – problems with families have an uncanny way of turning up when you could least do with them.

Your baby has an insatiable appetite for love and attention and relies totally on you and your partner. Naturally, the weight of this burden can be heavy to bear. So the baby's needs must be recognised as a priority.

You may have other children to look after and they are important too and may be very demanding, competing with the baby for your attention. There is also your partner who is probably your main support and you want to maintain a good relationship, despite the stress. Then there is the home – the housework, the shopping, the washing, the ironing, the cooking, the garden, the pets.

Lastly, although perhaps it should be top of the list, is your own physical and emotional well-being. You are very important because you are the key figure in the family, so if you are unwell or unhappy, everyone will suffer.

It is not surprising that many mothers feel overwhelmed by all these demands. You may feel that you ought to be 'superwoman' and be able to cope, uncomplaining, with everything. Things are hard enough with a new baby who is reasonably content. They can become far worse when a baby is crying or sleepless. It does not take much working out that there are going to have to be some compromises to help you survive this difficult time but what these compromises are will depend on you.

Take control

It is not uncommon for parents of crying babies to feel they are caught in a downward spiral with no control over their lives. The baby is unpredictable and that in itself is hard to cope with. Plans are made and cannot be carried out. Mothers in particular feel they are victims in a helpless and hopeless situation. It is harder still if the mother has always seen herself very much in control of circumstances.

If you see the baby as the fault – 'he is naughty' or 'he is getting at me', or yourself as the cause – 'I am a failure as a mother', you will tend to give up because you will feel that you have lost control. Think more positively. See the *situation* of having a crying baby (not uncommon – remember one in ten babies cry excessively) as the cause of your problems, and you and the baby as unfortunate, interdependent variables in the matter.

It is possible to make certain changes and improvements. You cannot always control the baby, but you can help the baby as best you know and you can reward yourself for being a good and caring parent. You can also plan a strategy to help you both.

Plan a strategy

There have been some drastic changes in your life and a great deal of physical and emotional upheaval. The ideas in this book are designed to build up your confidence which may have plummeted and to help you find your own solutions.

Plan some strategies, together with your partner if possible, and include some positive things to do, like seeing the health visitor regularly, getting out to meet other mothers and babies, organising a regular break from the baby, and keeping a diary of your baby's progress. For the moment, accept the way the baby is and see it is as creating only temporary problems.

Work out what your problems are and see what can be done about them. The previous Chapters and this Chapter will help. It is not possible to solve all the problems but you can start thinking about making improvements. It may require actually doing things to make changes, it may require asking other people to do things, or it may require a change in your outlook.

Do not set standards which you are not able to attain. They will only cause you added frustration. For example, don't plan to do all the washing, ironing and shopping in one day. Reduce your expectations of daily achievements and set realistic, simple goals, eg wash hair and prepare the dinner. If these are achieved, other tasks can be added one by one. If they are not achieved, be adaptable enough to change your plans to another day or abolish them altogether.

Hilary described her survival plan for her first baby who cried mainly in the afternoons and evenings for the first five months. 'I coped with it mainly by taking several walks a day. It never seemed as bad in the open, and by giving the baby to my husband at every opportunity, it didn't seem to affect him as much. He had much more patience with her and still has. I found that having just a few minutes to calm down by myself helped to keep my temper and enabled me to cope much better.' Her second baby was even more difficult and cried for 15 months, turning out to have a cow's milk allergy. This time, she found periods when the baby could lie without a nappy helped as well as 'several walks a day – the dog thought all her birthdays had come at once! We also gave the baby a dummy which calmed the screaming at night but he was seven months old before he'd take one so we had seven months to cope with beforehand. My husband and I used to take turns at the weekends to have a morning in bed to catch up on sleep and have some peace and quiet . . . I developed a sort of cut off switch which made it possible to keep the screaming in the background some of the time. I'm sure this was nature's way of making sure both the baby and I survived to see another day.'

Re-evaluate your baby's disposition every so often. Remember that your baby is changing all the time. The baby may be getting better – maybe not every day, but on the whole. It is unlikely to take place overnight, but you may be able to see some positive steps towards an improvement, for instance sleeping a bit longer at night, or taking less time to fall asleep. There is a real danger of giving the baby such a bad reputation, in your own mind and in justification to others, that you may find it difficult acknowledging that things are not quite as bad as they were. So try and be openminded about this.

Face and share your feelings

You may be feeling guilty, angry, resentful or just very unhappy. Face these feelings, however alien they are to you. Accept them as normal and understandable under the circumstances. There is no right or wrong way most of the time. Everyone makes mistakes and everyone has regrets. Put any regrets behind you.

Sharing your feelings with others is an important step to understanding and rationalising them. Your partner should probably be the first person to turn to, then perhaps family and friends, and hopefully other parents. You may find it helpful talking to your health visitor or GP and it will give your professional advisers the chance to hear that all is not well, as well as to reassure you at the same time.

If you find it difficult admitting your emotions to anyone close to you or to a professional adviser, share them with a support group, like CRY-SIS or Parents Anonymous (address and phone numbers in Appendix 1), or other family helplines which operate in some areas of the country – ask at your doctor's surgery or health clinic or library for details of local helplines.

It will be a great relief just talking about these feelings and hearing other people sympathise with you. Gillian has this advice for parents with a crying baby. 'My advice to parents in this situation would be don't blame yourself, it's not your fault you have a difficult baby; in the meantime, make every effort to meet other parents and have some social contact.'

The sound of your baby's crying may have a complex effect on you and could bring back unhappy nagging memories of your own childhood or sad occasions which you may not have come to terms with. You could start feeling very upset or depressed because of this, so it is even more important to talk to someone you can trust about all these complicated feelings.

Look after yourself

Women usually experience stress and pain during childbirth and afterwards it takes quite a few weeks for the body to recover from the upheaval and from stitches, scars and other problems, like sore breasts. Changes in hormone levels leave many mothers feeling low and tearful, finding it difficult to cope with the new baby. The mother's own physical and emotional needs are often her last consideration, but being a positive parent means giving yourself top priority.

Be good to yourself, particularly during this stressful phase and find time each day to relax. Do your post-natal exercises, or have a long bath or have your hair done, or whatever makes you feel good.

Do not forget to eat properly too. Many mothers exist on a rubbish diet through lack of time and enthusiasm. Particularly if you are breastfeeding, but even if you are not, eat regularly nutritious meals and snacks to maintain your stamina and health. Vitamin and mineral supplements may also help – ask your GP's or hospital or community dietician's advice if you are not sure what to take.

Try not to feel pressurised to lose weight as quickly as possible by dieting, which could affect your breastmilk. Don't compare yourself with the advertising stereotypes of a new mother – for most women these are far from the truth.

If you feel a mess, don't let it bother you. Give yourself permission to be a 'slob' for a few weeks until things are easier. You can explain this conscious decision to your partner, family and friends. It is important, however, that 'opting out' does not prevent you from going out or having visitors at home.

Try and get out every day with the baby even if it is just up the road and back. Try and have a regular break away from the baby, even if it is only for one hour a week. Ask your husband, relative or friend to babysit. Give yourself a real treat occasionally.

A friend of mine whose second baby had cried a great deal for the first six months was persuaded by her husband to spend a day at a 'health farm' whilst he took over the children. She went with a girlfriend and had a marvellous relaxing day, enjoying saunas and swims and being pampered and manicured. She realised afterwards that this day had provided a release of her built-up tensions and she felt set up to cope again.

Being good to yourself can also mean letting yourself be loved and mothered by others close to you. Allowing yourself to be helped means admitting to others that things are difficult. This is something many mothers find almost impossible to say.

Jane wrote of this dilemma: 'The most frightening part of the whole experience was my awareness that I was going to pieces. Sometimes, I had an almost physical sensation of my head exploding, or burning, to release all the tension. I was always either crying, in a furious rage or just overwhelmed with a pathetic sense of uselessness, futility and self pity. And yet I always had just enough energy to cover this up. My husband knew what state I was in, but most of my friends were shown my "I am coping" act, which was pretty exhausting to put on, so I went out less and less. I certainly asked people round less and less because the house was in utter chaos. I was ashamed of myself and frightened that there would be no end to it.'

Jane's act finally broke down when she went to her GP who was very sympathetic. 'I realised that he was concerned about *me* not the baby.' Her GP could only suggest that her husband took a week off work to give her a break. Jane continues 'In the end I went to my sister's for a week with both children. That week, I am quite certain, saved me from some sort of breakdown. She took all the children out in the afternoons so that I could catch up on sleep, and I did nothing at all except feed the baby. Once I had some energy back, I returned home with a completely different attitude. I asked for help from friends; I went out to friends's houses whenever I could, and I tried to stop feeling ashamed about constantly having to feed my baby wherever I went.'

Shock of your baby

If your expectations about your baby have been shattered, this would hardly be surprising, particularly for first-time parents. As Rhona put it 'I looked forward to my first child being born so much. I longed to have him to hold, to take for walks, to teach him all sorts of things. It came as a real bombshell when he was born, as at one to two days old, he lay awake in his cot in the hospital almost constantly. He then started crying most of the time and needed constant nursing.'

The *Parents Magazine* survey into crying babies found that 80% of the mothers who attended antenatal classes said the subject of unsettled babies was never discussed. Nearly four out of ten of the mothers in the survey were unprepared for the baby crying a lot. One of the recommendations of the survey called for antenatal teachers to give enough time to discussing how to cope with a crying baby.

People might say that nothing can prepare you for the experience of a crying baby, but I would disagree. Prior knowledge about the problem, how common it is, the possible causes, the possible remedies, how to get help for the baby and yourself can only result in parents coping better and blaming themselves far less. Unfortunately, parents receive little enough training for the important role of childcare in general, let alone dealing with any problems.

Your crying baby's arrival may shatter your plans as well as your expectations. Eileen had planned to go back to her office job after having the baby, but she says' 'There was no way I could.'

Isolation

Feeling isolated and alone with your crying baby is one of the hardest problems a parent has to face. First-time parents in particular may not have had the chance to build up a circle of friends in the home environment. For perhaps the first time in their lives they are spending most days without adult company.

Indeed, the *Parents Magazine* survey found that 92% of mothers spent up to 12 hours of every day on their own with the baby who was often crying but eight out of ten mothers felt better by talking about the problem. Social contact was very important from the letters I received in helping the mothers cope with the baby. Isolation and loneliness led to other problems, like depression, anger, lack of confidence and being overwhelmed.

Mothers often feel trapped into staying at home because they are embarrassed by the baby's crying in public. Vanessa says 'Eventually I could not go out to see people because as soon as I got there, she would scream the place down.' Alison too became more and more lonely with her crying baby as her husband worked long hours and she had no family to help her. She writes 'Whenever a friend did visit I would feel almost embarrassed by Laura's crying and then feel apologetic. It's hard to hold a conversation or make a coffee with a crying baby deafening the sound of your voice. As a result, I tended to avoid visits especially at suspect times of the day and this led me to feel very depressed and lonely.'

However difficult it is, it is important for you to make as much contact with other people as you can – the alternative is often to stay indoors with the baby crying. Of course, some days the effort will seem too great but try to get out as much as you can – every day if possible.

Combat loneliness

Here are some suggestions to help combat loneliness. Go out shopping every day, walking the baby in the pram or buggy if possible. Go to the health clinic once a week. Ask another mother you usually see there to come to your house for a coffee and set a date. Ask the local National Childbirth Trust branch (address in Appendix 1) about post-natal support groups, where mothers with similar aged babies can get together at one another's homes. Occasionally they can supply support on a one-to-one basis. Sometimes, branches arrange evening meetings too with guest speakers on subjects of interest. If you are breastfeeding, perhaps you could join the local branch of La Leche League or the Association of Breastfeeding Mothers (addresses in Appendix 1). Go to a Mother and Baby or a Toddler group. Your health visitor should know of one. Stop a neighbour you have seen with a pram and ask her around for a cup of tea.

Get out in the evenings or at weekends with some old friends, who perhaps do not have any children. Go out with your partner with the baby at weekends to visit friends or family or just to the park or out somewhere in the car or on the bus. Go out with your partner alone if you can for an occasional evening or an afternoon at weekends. There may be a local babysitting circle of mothers who sit for one another, or you may find a teenager happy to sit for a small sum. You may be lucky enough to have a relative or friend dying to look after the baby for a few hours – no matter how much the baby cries. Take up any offers.

Single parents can also join special parent groups, like Gingerbread (address in Appendix 1) and may meet other parents in similar situations with whom they could arrange mutual babysitting to give one another a break.

Talk to everyone about the baby. You will be surprised to find out how many other parents have had a crying baby. 'Even the gasman had one' said one mother. Talk about your problems to your health visitor and GP. Ask them about local facilities. Contact a support group like CRY-SIS, where it is possible to talk anonymously if you wish to another parent who has had similar experiences.

If you feel lonely at home, turn on the television or radio. Local radio news stations are especially interesting with regular features and current affairs programmes. It will help you feel part of the outside world and give you a distraction from the baby.

If you feel lonely at night, try a 'walkman' portable radio or cassette player, for music or night chat shows, and you need not disturb anyone else by listening through earphones.

Even though Melanie found it difficult going out shopping with her baby whose screaming seemed to turn everyone's attention, she still has this advice for other mums 'Don't stay indoors on your own but join a mum and toddler group and go out as much as possible. I found it really helps.'

Exhaustion

Many of the mothers who wrote to me described how they felt 'exhausted', 'worn out' or 'done-in'. Some described how the tiredness affected their ability to think clearly about anything and they easily became confused. Others described difficulty concentrating, for instance on driving a car.

Deprivation of sleep is a well-known form of torture and it may seem that your body and mind are being tormented. You may experience aches and pains or feel light-headed – these are quite normal under the circumstances. It may be possible to catch a few hours sleep altogether but it will almost certainly be broken up into short intervals. Sally-Ann, who had a particularly sleepless baby, writes 'I dreamt of more than four hours sleep, not consecutive hours – just four hours in any one night.'

Surprisingly enough you body can adjust to less sleep or broken periods of sleep but you are unlikely to feel very fit. The easiest solution is to accept the situation and work out a strategy so that you rest, if not sleep, as much as possible and do not put too many demands on yourself.

First-time mothers should take the opportunity to sleep in as long as possible in the morning – go back to sleep if the baby sleeps after the morning feed, or just lie in bed resting, reading the paper, having breakfast, or listening to the radio or watching television. I hardly ever got dressed before midday but at least I felt a little more human. Do not worry about anything else, like the housework – your rest is more important.

Mothers with older children will probably feel even more tired and have to get up to see to the family in the morning. If possible, get your partner to wash and dress older children, or encourage them to do this themselves, as well as preparing their own breakfast if they are old enough. Of course, you will have to see to a toddler, but afterwards you may be able to go back to bed, whilst the child plays with some toys on the bedroom floor and the baby hopefully sleeps. Take up all offers from friends of lifts for your children to playschool or school. You can make it up to them when your nights improve.

During the night, share the responsibility of seeing to the baby with your partner if possible. Maybe at weekends you could take it in turns to have a lie-in, or let your partner take over for a whole day occasionally and either go out or if you are breastfeeding, let your partner just bring the baby to you for feeds so that you can stay in bed catching up on sleep.

Sally's baby was still crying a great deal when she wrote to me, and she described how she was trying to cope with exhaustion. 'I think somehow you have to battle on even though, as I feel now, I'm going to drop dead from exhaustion. You have to find a sort of inner strength to cope and above all to try and stay calm and not to let it get on top of you. Whenever I get the chance I escape into town on Saturdays and leave my husband to cope.' Sally went on to say 'We have persuaded my mother-in-law to have Adam for us for the weekend, because I am so desperate for a break.'

Like Sally, you might be able to leave the baby with someone else for a weekend or for a day, so that you have a complete break from the crying. If you are breastfeeding, it may be possible to save enough expressed breastmilk, which can be frozen or kept in the fridge for up to 24 hours.

If this is difficult to arrange, consider using a childminder to have the baby on a regular basis – like once a week for an afternoon. Leave bottles of expressed breastmilk or formula milk for a bottlefed baby, and enjoy the break. Ask your health visitor to recommend a local childminder, who will be experienced and capable of coping, even if the baby cries. If the baby takes a while to settle down with this arrangement, do not give up on it. It is a good idea for the baby to learn to accept another carer occasionally, and I am sure you will not regret it.

Try making an arrangement with another mother to have each other's baby once a week, so that you can both have a break. It may not be as hard as you imagine, looking after two babies (mothers of twins have to all the time) and your baby may be more settled in another house, with the distraction of new faces.

During normal days, lie down or sit down with your feet up for at least five minutes every hour or two. Practise the relaxation exercises you were taught at ante-natal classes. Here is one popular method of relaxation. Lie down, close your eyes and breathe evenly and slowly. Starting with your feet, clench and then relax your muscles, working up through your body – your legs, the muscles of your pelvic floor and stomach, your chest, shoulders, arms, hands, neck and ending with the muscles of your face. Go back, mentally, over all your muscles checking that they are still relaxed. Some people find it helps to play soft music in the background, whilst others find it useful to visualise a beautiful scene, like a warm tropical beach. This method of relaxation has been known to send some people to sleep.

Try to make life easier for yourself during the day and night. Get some help in the home if possible or take up any offers of help. Cut down on housework and keep meals simple but nutritious. Get your partner to do the shopping at weekends or in the evenings. Make life simpler at night by bringing the baby into your bed or pushing the cot next to your bed and dropping down the side, so that you can just roll over and feed the baby when necessary.

Resentment, anger and frustration

Feelings of resentment are quite understandable in the build-up of tension and exhaustion the parents of crying babies often experience. The noise of the crying which cannot always be switched off may result in intense feelings of anger and frustration – anger at the baby and frustration at not being able to turn the crying off.

Other resentments can surface too – like the resentment felt by many mothers that their partner can escape from the baby by going to work, or resentment against other mothers with easier babies.

More than half of the mothers who wrote to me admitted to coming very close to actually hurting the baby. Most of them were able to cope with this frightening feeling by getting away from the baby for a short period whilst they calmed down. This served to act as a safety valve. Maggie explained: 'The hall door was my best friend when I was really desperate in those early weeks. When I reached screaming pitch, I'd put her out in the hall in her pram, slam the door shut, have a fag and a cup of coffee, pull myself together, and then much calmed, enter into battle anew.'

Sally-Ann came to the end of her tether one day when the baby would not stop screaming despite everything she had tried. After an hour and a half she did not dare pick the baby up from his cot for fear of hurting him. 'I was standing over him screaming at him myself. I opened the window at one point and hoped someone in the shop downstairs would hear me.' Two hours later when a friend arrived, the baby was still crying and Sally-Ann was still shouting and crying herself. Together they managed to calm the baby, but the memory of this event still distresses her. Things did not improve with the baby. Sally-Ann continues 'I didn't have much help at this time. We knew no one locally. Our parents who only saw us occasionally said he was a lovely baby and got quite upset if I said I was worried about battering him. I didn't dare tell the health visitor – social services would have taken him away, so we just went on. My husband couldn't do anything. I didn't blame him for the crying, but I certainly took it out on him. I don't think anyone realised that when they said "What a lovely baby" and I replied "You can keep him" I was serious.'

Finally, Sally-Ann and her husband were helped by several

concerned friends who for nearly a month took it in turns, sometimes travelling over 30 miles, to go to their house and take over the baby during the night, whilst the parents slept. Sally-Ann was passed caring, and the friends decided to let the baby 'scream it out', which after a week worked. The baby slept better at night and became 'a truly delightful baby' during the day.

Jeannette found another way of coping with her feelings of anger. 'The only thing that saved me from doing her damage was my mum. She didn't live too far away and went out of her way to come round every other day for at least an hour or two so I could get some sleep. Also, one weekend out of every month, I would take the baby to her house on Saturday, leave her crying there, and not go back until lunchtime on Sunday. She would always be crying when I arrived and my mum was totally worn out, although she'd never say.'

Here are some other positive suggestions of helping with feelings of resentment and anger.

If you fear harming the baby, talk to someone about how you feel – ideally it should be your health visitor or GP, but it could be a trusted friend or relative or a support group, like CRY-SIS. Most will understand how you feel and give you plenty of support and reassurance, and it will certainly help talking about it.

If you get really angry, put the baby safely in its cot and leave the room for a few minutes to calm down. It may help to get out into the garden or walk down the road for a few minutes.

Phone up a relative or friend. Go out with the baby to see someone you can talk to, or ask someone to have the baby for a while for you. If a neighbour or friend realises how desperate you feel, they would almost certainly help you.

Have *one* alcoholic drink if it helps you calm down, or try a herbal remedy or tea.

Take your feelings out on an object. Try punching a pillow or cushion really hard. Slam the door hard. Go to the bottom of the garden or get into a car, shut the windows, and yell! Try some energetic sport where you can slam a ball, like tennis or squash. Try jogging, or walking fast, swimming, or any other form of exercise.

If you are just feeling frustrated, try taking up another interest. Sometimes, it is possible to join day-time classes and leave the baby in a creche, or maybe you could join an evening class and let your partner take over. You might be able to learn a useful new skill or improve an old one. Set aside time every day, even if it is only a half an hour, to do something you enjoy, like reading, sketching, painting, cake decorating, writing letters, doing a puzzle, gardening, knitting or sewing.

Ask in the library about local groups for mothers at home, like the National Housewives Register, who meet together and have speakers and topics of interest.

For some mothers, the answer is to return to work part-time or full-time, and using a childminder if there are no creche facilities. It is often possible to keep a former job open under maternity leave regulations. It might be possible to find another job by looking out in the papers and registering at a Job Centre.

Feeling depressed

Fourteen mothers who wrote to me said they suffered from depression, usually because the baby was constantly crying and they were so exhausted. Sharon described how she felt. 'Up until he was about six months old, I was desperately tired all the time and depressed. He cried so much that even when he was asleep, I could still hear his screams ringing in my ears, so that I was never able to relax at all and was lucky if I got just a few hours sleep each night.'

Sometimes, rather than the baby crying a great deal, the mother is suffering from post-natal depression, but she does not realise this and blames the baby for her tiredness. The mother's tolerance level will be lower to any crying or sleeplessness. It can be a combination of having a crying baby and suffering from post-natal depression.

Post-natal depression is thought by some medical authorities to be the result of the dramatic hormonal changes that take place after birth. Other professionals believe it is caused by psychological difficulties in adjusting to motherhood, and still others say it is a response to the everyday stresses of looking after a baby.

The most common form of post-natal depression experienced by over half of mothers, is the baby or maternity blues, which come on a few days after the baby is born and are characterised by tearfulness, mood-swings, getting upset by remarks and becoming easily anxious about the baby. The blues last for a few days only.

When depression does not go away quickly, or goes then returns, this is called post-natal depression and affects perhaps 15% of mothers. Some of the symptoms are endless deep exhaustion, apathy and extreme irritability – usually directed at the mother's partner, baby or other children. Mothers may sit around all day, unable to cope with the simplest chores and unwilling to go out. They may lose interest in their appearance, especially if they feel they are overweight, and they may experience cravings for sugary foods. There is a yearning for sleep and a depressed mother can sleep all day – unlike other forms of depression where sleep is difficult – but the mother still remains tired and weary.

Gillian described how depressed she felt. 'I began having anxiety attacks and obsessive thoughts about illness, death and the feeling that life was meaningless. It wasn't until long afterwards that I recognised these as classic symptoms of post-natal depression, so I didn't ask for help, I thought I was going mad!' As Gillian's letter suggests, other symptoms of post-natal depression can be panic attacks, as well as sweats, shaking, aches and pains, lack of concentration, lack of interest in sex and loss of confidence.

This type of depression can be helped by reducing stress from all sources – difficult for the mother of a crying baby – and by a sufficient and balanced intake of wholefoods. Food supplements that are currently being investigated to see if they help are vitamin B6, zinc, evening primrose oil and amino acids. A variety of biochemical changes may cause or worsen post-natal depression, including changes in brain chemistry or slow adrenal or thyroid functioning, and a few women have been treated with the relevant hormonal substances. Usually mothers who seek help from their GPs are given antidepressant drugs and many felt these helped to start them on the road to recovery.

Post-natal depression can last longer than the problems which seemed to start it as Ruth found. 'Even though things got easier with my son after four months, the depression I've suffered is only just receding. It's only now I can look at my son and feel real love, the bond that everyone tells you should happen automatically. I still get bad days when I'd like to sit in a corner and cry all day.'

There seems to be a link between post-natal depression and premenstrual tension. Women who have suffered from premenstrual tension have been found to be more prone to post-natal depression, whilst some mothers who never experienced premenstrual tension develop it after the birth. Dr. Katharina Dalton has worked for some 30 years on the hormonal causes of premenstrual tension and post-natal depression and she has successfully treated women with natural progesterone.[1] Some other doctors offer similar treatment. In her book, Depression after Childbirth, Dr. Dalton describes how the dramatic drop in hormone levels after birth contrasts with high levels during pregnancy and says that often women affected by post-natal depression felt elated and better than usual during the last months of pregnancy.

Other authorities feel the most effective treatment of post-natal depression is counselling.[2] Talk to your GP or health visitor if you are feeling depressed or if you recognise the symptoms described. It is important to talk to other sympathetic people too. Ruth found it difficult finding anyone who understood at the time and writes 'What would have helped? Someone to phone up on a regular basis to see how I was. I used to get so depressed that I would phone friends up to see how they were, waiting for them to ask how I was!'

Special support groups, like the Association for Post-Natal Illness, MAMA or CRY-SIS (addresses in Appendix 1) will be able to provide a listening ear from someone who understands what you are going through. The National Childbirth Trust have general post-natal support groups that supply specific expertise in supporting those with post-natal depression. Some areas of the country have special schemes, like Home Start (address in Appendix 1) which will provide help from other parents on a voluntary basis or just company in your home. Ask your health visitor for information about this.

Guilt

The majority of parents with a crying baby experience a great deal of guilt.

The mothers who contributed to this book often mentioned feeling guilty: for not being able to stop the crying and make the baby happier; for resenting the baby; for not having enough time for other children or their partner; for not being able to keep up with the housework. If they wanted to get away from the baby, they felt guilty.

If they left the baby with someone, they felt guilty. If they went back to work, they felt guilty.

The guilt trap is only likely to make you feel more depressed and less confident. Try and assure yourself that you are not to blame for your baby's crying and that hundreds of other parents feel the same way as you. Put any guilt feelings behind you, or accept them as quite normal in your situation.

Loss of confidence

Discovering positive and negative aspects of your baby helps you learn and develop your confidence. Unfortunately it may seem that there are very little positive elements about your baby, so your confidence may become very low. You could find yourself very unsure of how to look after the baby – although, your baby is likely to respond better to a confident approach from its parents. Loss of confidence does nothing to break up the vicious circle of a crying baby and distressed parents.

Lack of confidence with the baby can start affecting other decisions and your whole outlook. First-time parents are particularly susceptible as they have no experience of bringing up a baby. One mother considered herself very lucky that her crying baby was her second child 'so I did have enough confidence to know that I was doing nothing wrong.'

As well as these problems, the realisation of your responsibility and the fear that the crying will never end, can present a frightening prospect. Parents often feel out of control and utterly inadequate too.

One solution to help these problems is to start thinking positively, stop blaming yourself or the baby, and start acknowledging that you are doing a great job under very difficult conditions. Every time the baby is pacified, congratulate *yourself* on achieving this, not good fortune. Every time your baby cannot be pacified, do not see this as your fault, as you will have tried everything you know to help.

Avoid tasks that you are unlikely to be able to complete as this will only lead to further frustration and loss of confidence. Every time you manage to achieve a target, like baking a cake or making a phone call to a friend, congratulate yourself.

Take every opportunity to enjoy the baby and really wallow in the knowledge that the baby loves you unconditionally.

Start making your own decisions about your life and the baby. Try not to let other people take over from you. It does not help that the treatment of mothers during pregnancy, childbirth and aftercare in hospital does little to inspire confidence. Mothers tend to be discouraged from making decisions, asking questions or feeling in control of events. It is easy for new parents to feel that 'other people know best'. However, you know best and it is your baby! Ask the advice of professionals – in fact, use their knowledge and services to the full – but make sure that it is *you* who makes the final decision.

Try not to look into the future with dread either. Your baby will get over this stage, and it may start happening tomorrow or next week or next month. In the meantime, help the baby and yourself and be assured that your baby will get better.

Feeling sorry for the baby

Parents often feel desperately sorry for their crying baby. Barbara described this helplessness and heartache. 'My main feelings in response to Steven's apparent misery have been distress that he wasn't happy . . . I assumed that with feeding on demand, lots of love and cuddles, things to look at and, eventually, play with, a baby would be happy. When Steven was *not* what could be called a happy, contented baby, I felt an utter failure.'

It is quite revealing that in the *Parents Magazine* survey into crying babies, more fathers felt sorry for the baby then for their partners. If you feel that your own problems have been underestimated or overlooked amongst all the concern over the baby, now is the time to talk this over with your partner. It may be that your partner is away so much that he does not realise the effect the baby is having on you, and when you are together with the baby, you will almost certainly not feel as distressed as you do when alone.

Raphael, a father of two children, who were not crying babies, wrote about his interesting ideas on crying in children and how he and his wife coped with normal tears. Raphael felt that it was important to let babies and children cry, in the security of their parents' arms and love. He remembered only too well how he had often been prevented from crying as a boy, like many other children. He felt that because times of distress had been suppressed, many adults carry around unreleased tensions about showing emotion, which were worsened by the sounds of their own child crying. Raphael felt that parents should not discourage their children from crying if they seemed to want to and he ended his letter with this comment 'If your child is happily getting on with life, you must be a good parent. If she's crying her eyes out in your arms, you must be a good parent too. Either way, you win. And your children certainly will too.'

Coping with the home

A crying baby requires special attention. There is often little time for ordinary household chores and the mother will probably have little energy left too. It is particularly difficult for a mother who likes keeping her home clean and tidy, but remember that this is a temporary period, and you will be able to get your home straight again in the near future.

Carol's comments show the tension that mounting housework causes. 'I was so exhausted that I couldn't do any housework and I was in tears every night when my husband got home from work.'

Here is one way of helping with housework which may work for you. Write down all the chores that you usually undertake every day, once a week, or once a month, from the simplest to the most complicated. Then look hard at the list and rearrange them into priority order. Forget about low priority tasks which can wait until the baby is older (I never like cleaning the cooker much anyway). Then write down a list of all the really essential chores which you feel must be done every day: include in this list sterilising bottles, keeping the food area in the kitchen clean, and sterilising terry nappies. Then make a list of the chores you would like to complete once a week, keeping this to a minimum.

If you still find it hard coping or if the house is getting on your nerves, consider employing some help in the home for this short period, if you can possibly afford it. It would be worth doing without some little luxury to afford this help. For very little money, someone could achieve in two hours what will take you a week. If there are special circumstances, like twins or a Caesarian section, it may be possible to get a Home Help provided by the local Social Services.

Sometimes, this help can be provided free or subsidised. Ask your health visitor about the local policy on this.

You may have a friend or relative who has offered to help in any way. Some mothers find it more useful to have extra help in the home rather than with the baby, so take up any offers. There will always be something that needs doing, like the ironing, which could be taken away and brought back a few days later.

To make life easier, consider using disposable nappies. There seems to be very little difference in actual cost between disposable and terry nappies, which need to be sterilised and washed.

It is also sometimes possible to find shops or individuals who sell home cooking for the freezer. It may be a little more expensive than cooking yourself, but is a great time-saver or stand-by when you want to treat yourself to a tasty dish.

One mother found it helped her to cope better with the home if she cleaned and dusted her living room each day, whilst she totally ignored the rest of the house.

Coping with other children

Parents with other children will feel torn between them and the baby who is noisily demanding attention. It can be a very difficult time for the family.

One mother wrote about how the crying baby affected her relationship with her young toddler. 'Throughout all this, I was very irritable. My daughter was neglected and spent a lot of her time at my mother's house whilst I walked the streets with Tom airing his lungs in the pram. My poor daughter suffered most. The baby would get me so wound up I would take it out on her. I couldn't hit a baby but I could slap a two year old. Funnily enough she has always adored him. She never resents him and has tried to amuse him and help me since he was born.'

Other children do seem to weather the storm. Try and give some special responsibilities to them or let them help you with the baby so that they feel more grown up. Try and give some special time every day to another child, preferably without the baby, even if it is only a few minutes. Try not to be too irritated by any lapses into babyish behaviour or being demanding, as this is only an indication of the child's insecurity and jealousy of the newcomer.

On the other hand, sometimes it does an older child good to see that things are normal at home. When I first came home with my crying baby son, my two year old daughter played up for quite a few weeks. Eventually, I lost my temper with her and told her off. She immediately settled down, obviously realising that mum had not changed at all.

Strains on your marriage

Although your partner is likely to be your biggest source of support, any marriage can suffer under the strain of a crying baby. Resentments and tensions build up and arguments and irritability with one another are very common.

Maggie described how her husband was unemployed and demoralised himself, often losing his temper with the baby and walking out which left her to cope alone. She came to resent him having the choice whether to stay and calm the baby or leave.

Fathers may work longer hours to stay away from the home or to meet financial commitments on one salary. Many mothers feel that their husbands could do more to support them or help more with the baby or the housework.

Some fathers become jealous of the time the mother spends with the baby and start to feel shut out. They might find it hard forming a bond with the baby who also seems to reject them. The mother may be snappy too through exhaustion or depression.

Try and involve your partner with the baby as much as you can. Try not to snatch the baby away because you do not think he is doing it right. Give him the chance to learn too.

For many couples, sexual relationships are reduced or non-existent during this time – through tiredness, constant interruptions, or lack of interest. If this is the case, try not to worry about it as things will return to normal eventually. Consult your GP if you are really worried about lack of libido. Use other opportunities to cuddle and be close together.

If your relationship is suffering, the way around the dilemma is to realise what is happening to you both and talk to each other about how you both feel. Put over your points of view and see if you can work out ways of helping each other. Like any conflict, compromises will have to be made on both sides.

The important thing is that you work together as a team if possible and agree decisions together. One couple may find it acceptable for the husband to get up to the baby at night, whereas another couple will not. There is no hard and fast rule. If you have worked it out together and both feel satisfied, then it is right for you.

If you really cannot work things out, do not let the situation ruin your partnership. Consult a Marriage Guidance counsellor or similar acceptable mediator, who may be able to help.

Give yourself some time alone together if possible, to go out in the evening or at the weekend, leaving the baby with someone else you trust. Treat yourselves to a meal out or a good film; you will feel much better for it.

One mother voiced the comments of several others. Although there had been a rift between her and her husband whilst the baby was crying so much, in the long run it brought them closer together.

Coping with other people

Many people seem to feel they have the right to pass comments or give advice to a new mother and her baby, almost as if you have both become public property. I sometimes wonder if they sense your lack of confidence or vulnerability and take advantage of it.

Some people's reaction can be very encouraging while others can be very hurtful. Here are a few examples:

Astonished: 'I've never seen a baby like this.'

Sympathiser: 'Mine was just the same.'

Patroniser: 'You first-time mums worry about every little cry, DEAR.'

Advice-giver: 'Try this . . . or this . . . it never fails.'

Self-righteous: 'Of course, we never had any problems.'

Disbeliever: 'Surely not, she's perfectly all right now.'

Shocked: 'The baby must be ill.'

Accusor: 'You must be doing something wrong.' or 'Calm down, you're making him cry.'

And what about the old lady who stops you in the street and suggests that you feed the baby, when of course you just have. Or the kind soul who shouts at the top of her voice 'Someone's baby is crying!' when you have stood in the queue in the greengrocer's for ten minutes and are the next one to be served. (Didn't she know that you heard the baby start crying eight minutes ago but tried to ignore it, otherwise no one is going to have any dinner tonight.)

How much notice you take of remarks and advice, which are often contradictory, goes back to confidence again. It is easy for other people to offer solutions when they are not in the situation. It is also difficult to really understand unless you have experienced a crying, sleepless baby. So, consider any advice that sounds helpful, and ignore the remarks and advice that upsets you.

If anyone asks you why the baby cries so much, tell them the baby has got tummy ache and this condition is very common in small babies . . . didn't they know?

Notes
1 *Depression after childbirth*. Dr. Katharine Dalton, Oxford University Press, 1980.
2 *Taking post-natal depression seriously*. J.L. Cox and J.M. Holden. Health Visitor, June 1986, Vol. 59, 180–182.

8

How the medical profession can help

If your baby is crying more than you think is normal or sleeping very little, medical advisers are available who can help.

You may not have had much contact with doctors and nurses before having the baby, so you may find it strange asking for help and feel silly asking questions which are so important and confusing to you, and to which the answers seem so simple.

Remember that if you are a first-time parent, you are learning how to care for a child and many things are new and uncertain. You need help and reassurance. In more family-orientated societies, someone would always be on hand to show you how to do things and you would have had more contact with babies before having your own. In our society, parents' own mothers and family often lack confidence in handling new babies or offering advice, having forgotten many of the practical aspects of babycare.

Parents with other children still need advice and help with a crying baby and may be shy about asking for it, feeling they should know what to do. Experience with other babies may not have prepared you for this one!

Asking for help and advice is not an admission of failure. Quite the contrary – it is a sensible step to improve the situation, check the baby's health and help you cope better.

From my experience of talking to parents of crying babies, the ones who find it hardest to cope are the ones who automatically thought they would be able to cope – doctors, nurses, midwives, health visitors, nursery nurses and nannies! Indeed, five of the parents who wrote to me were trained health care professionals.

Maggie, a doctor, writes: 'I could tell he was not ill – he put on weight and developed normally, but I was quite ignorant of the fact that some babies just cried excessively. I had always expected to be a calm coping mother and felt enormous guilt and shame when I realised that I was (in my eyes) failing to give my baby what he

Checklist of baby's symptoms

Crying

Type of cry eg sharp, rhythmic, whiny, scream.

Intensity.

Daily amount of crying.

Time of day eg any pattern.

How you normally pacify.

Sleep

Usual pattern of sleeping.

Where baby sleeps best.

What happens when baby wakes in day or night.

Feeding

Poor appetite, always hungry.

Problems with breastfeeding.

Nipple soreness, problems with breasts, etc.

Problems giving bottle, type of bottle, teats.

Frequent hiccups.

Excessive wind.

Apparent pain during or after feeding.

Any adverse reaction to foods or drinks – by baby or eaten by breastfeeding mother.

Vomiting, bringing back milk

Amount.

When it occurs.

Projectile (shooting across room) or dribbling from mouth.

Colour of vomit, presence of blood or mucus.

Stools (take a dirty nappy with you to show doctor)

Number of bowel movements a day.

Diarrhoea or loose stools.

Constipation or pain passing bowel movement.

Colour; presence of blood, undigested food, mucus.

Urine

Strong or smelly.

Pain passing urine.

Pain

Areas which seems painful.

Movements of legs or arms which seem to cause pain.

Soreness or swelling

Areas which are red and/or swollen.

Nappy rash.

Skin

Areas of dryness, flaky skin.

Rashes, spots, itchiness, bleeding.

Sweaty skin, hot or cold skin.

needed. My health visitor was marvellous but a bit uneasy at offering advice to a doctor.' Another mother writes: 'I blamed myself at first for Nicoll's crying, thinking I should have been able to comfort him and stop the crying. Afterall, I am a trained nursery nurse and ought to know what to do. Sadly, no textbooks prepared me for this.'

Checklist of baby's symptoms – *continued*

Irritation with nappies, clothes, plastic pants.

Unusually pale skin.

Cold or cough

Runny nose, green mucus.

Frequent colds, sore throat or ear infections.

Sneezing.

Frequent coughing and type of cough.

Breathing

Wheezy chest, rattly breathing.

Panting.

Fast, shallow breathing.

Gasping, choking, erratic breathing or difficulty breathing.

Bad breath.

Head-banging or cot rocking

Possible symptoms of headache.

Temperature

Record it using a child's thermometer which you place on child's brow.

Hearing and sight

Hears you come in room, does not seem to hear.

Easily startled.

Does not seem to focus well (new-borns cannot focus more than a few inches). Does not follow movements of finger.

Weight gain

Discuss this with health visitor or GP.

General disposition

Tense and serious.

Generally cranky.

Happy until feeding or after feeding.

Prefers lying in cot to being held.

Wants to be held or carried constantly.

Likes or dislikes movement and rocking.

Easily upset, easily startled.

Throws arms back when picked up.

Has good days and bad days, has only bad days.

Prefers being at home, prefers going out.

Happy until late afternoon.

Happy during day, cries at night; sleeps well, unhappy during day.

Only wants mother, father.

Who to ask for help

Routine advice about the baby's development and care should be sought from your health visitor. In the early weeks, a visiting midwife may also be able to advise you. You may want to contact the maternity hospital where the baby was born. For medical advice and further reassurance, consult your GP or the doctor at your local health clinic. For more specialist help, a referral to a hospital paediatrician (child specialist) is possible. In some areas, it may also be possible to be referred to a crying baby clinic. What you can expect from these advisers is described in this Chapter.

How to ask for help

The medical professional do not seem to like having a diagnosis made for them, but it does help them diagnose any problems if you are specific. So, before you go to see your health visitor, GP or other professional, write down a list of all the relevant points you would like to discuss. To help you, use the checklist of possible symptoms on page 110. Take a diary too, as it is often difficult to remember in detail what has been happening over a period of time.

A good professional adviser will listen carefully to what you have to say; after all, you know the baby better than anyone. Make sure that you understand the answers to your questions or if you are explained something new. If you are still confused, ask to have the point clarified. Make sure too that your anxieties about the baby are reassured as much as possible.

Refer to your list of questions so that you do not leave the surgery or clinic without asking all of them. If you are particularly worried or intimidated by your adviser's attitude Ruth, a trained nurse, has this advice. 'When trying to convince a GP or the health visitor about a problem try to get your husband to go along too as much more notice will be taken of someone different from the mother.' Some mothers find it helpful to take a relative (like their own mother, sister or aunt) with them, or a friend or neighbour. The accompanying person should be supportive and, if possible, non-aggressive as this could make matters worse. Taking someone with you can give you the confidence to be more assertive about your anxieties and problems.

Do not be surprised either if you are asked some probing questions about yourself. Although you are probably only asking for advice about the baby, health professionals will be concerned about the effects of the baby's behaviour on you. They may also want to establish whether it is the baby who is the problem or perhaps the mother's depression.

Five years ago, one mother lamented on her GP's reaction to her crying baby: 'What the hell do you expect me to do about it?' Fortunately, doctors are becoming more sympathetic and sensitive about crying and sleepless babies. There have been a number of articles in journals and papers discussing factors which cause crying in babies. There is also a growing acceptance that allergies can sometimes account for crying and sleeplessness.

Nevertheless, you may still come across comments which seem to imply that you are somehow causing the crying, through worrying too much or being neurotic. These sorts of comments are very unhelpful as they cause great harm to a mother's confidence, as well as not giving her advice on how to cope. Vanessa found a lack of interest to her crying baby from her professional advisers. She writes 'I asked my health visitor, doctor and clinic for help and they all said vague things like "Give her gripe water" or "She's perfectly healthy" or "Some babies do cry". Vanessa felt particularly let down by her health visitor who did not seem to appreciate how she felt.

On the other hand, Carole found that persevering with her advisers proved worthwhile with the problem. Her health visitor was helpful and made some useful suggestions.

Some advisers confidently tell parents that at 'six weeks' or 'three months' the crying will pass. They are trying to help parents see the period of unsettledness as temporary and that there is an end in sight. Unfortunately, however, it can be an unhelpful promise to some parents who do not know how they will survive another night, let alone another few weeks! Also, if the crying continues beyond the expected date, the parents' moral can plummet.

Sometimes, different advisers give different advice on the management of the problem or opinions of the cause, which the parents find very confusing. Sometimes, a GP and health visitor do not work well together, and the parents find themselves in the middle of an internal conflict. The answer may be to stick with one professional who you feel you can trust.

Many professionals make parents feel that there is a right and a wrong way – they do this to avoid confusing you with endless possibilities and to make you feel more confident with their advice. However, this attitude may inhibit the development of confidence in your own decision-making. Some decisions are virtually made for you, eg if the baby needs antibiotics to combat an infection. Other decisions should be made by you with the advice and help of specialists. Experience often shows you that there is no right or wrong way – what is right for another baby may be wrong for yours. Being flexible is one of the keys to coping with a crying baby.

Consult your GP

If you are becoming concerned about the baby's health or your own health, consult your General Practitioner (GP). Mention everything that you have noticed, however, trivial. Mention too how you feel – for instance, any tiredness, depression, or anxiety.

Doctors often feel just as helpless as the parents when presented with a crying or sleepless baby. They cannot prescribe a medicine for the crying. A drug called Merbentyl used to be commonly prescribed to help colic but it is not now recommended for babies under six months. The doctor may offer to prescribe sedatives or sleep inducing drugs for the baby (see page 120) and sometimes for you too. Discuss these options fully first.

Other than this, your GP should examine the baby and ask pertinent questions. You can run through any symptoms which you consider unusual using the checklist on page 110. Make sure that the baby is examined thoroughly, including the baby's ears which can be very painful if inflamed. If your baby has not been examined for a few weeks, ask your GP to do this and explain that it will put your mind at rest.

If you find the time available in a busy surgery is insufficient to discuss the matter properly, ask the receptionist to make your next appointment a longer one.

You may feel a fraud complaining about the baby's crying, particularly if the baby behaves impeccably in the consulting room. Doctors are well aware of this fact. If you take with you a specific list of symptoms and questions you want to ask, a diary over the last few days or weeks, and maybe your partner, or sympathetic relative or friend, you will feel confident about voicing your concern.

Many GPs are supportive and sympathetic, and they will encourage parents to go and see them whenever they want further reassurance. Others are less helpful and do not seem to understand the pressures of the situation. If your GP is unsympathetic, try another doctor in the same practice or consider changing your GP.

When my first crying baby was little, my GP was unsupportive, giving me a lecture about colic but making me feel I was wasting his valuable time. By the time my second baby came along, we had moved and my next GP was very sympathetic and helpful. I remember seeing him when the baby was about nine weeks old and the same evening he called around to our house on his way home from a busy surgery and numerous housecalls, just to see how the baby was. The next morning before his surgery, he phoned up to see what sort of night we had had. Then, he sent us to the local hospital to take an X-ray of the baby to check for a hernia. The hospital did this and kept us in for tests for a few days. It was a great relief to feel that my doctor was supporting me and that the baby was being thoroughly checked. The diagnosis? 'An awful, crying baby', but nothing seemed wrong.

If things are not improving with your baby, at some stage you may wish to ask for a referral to a paediatrician. Some GPs hold back from this as they know how busy hospitals are and they hope that the problem will soon resolve itself. However, if you feel particularly anxious about the baby's health or if you feel the problem has continued for a long time, you can insist on a referral.

If the baby's health has been checked or is not in doubt, your GP may be able to refer you to a crying baby clinic – ask whether this is possible.

Consult your health visitor

All babies are allocated a health visitor. She is a trained nurse, usually with several years experience, including midwifery nursing. On top of this, she will have undertaken a further period of training in health visiting.

Your health visitor will operate from a clinic or health centre, sometimes in conjunction with a GP, sometimes covering a geographical area.

You will receive a visit from your health visitor shortly after you return home with the baby. From then on, she may visit regularly, tailing off visits once all seems to be going well, or she may only visit occasionally, perhaps if she is in the area, or has not seen you for a while. Your health visitor will hold a clinic, usually once a week, and you will be encouraged to take the baby to the clinic, have the baby weighed, and discuss any problems with the health visitor. There is an informal and friendly atmosphere and you will be able to talk to other mothers with similar aged babies.

Unfortunately, in some clinics it is not possible to talk to the health visitor in private should you want to. Also, it may be a very busy clinic and you may feel that you have not had enough time to talk over your problems fully. If this is the case, or if you just find it difficult getting to the clinic, telephone your health visitor and ask her to come and see you at home. She will probably come as soon as she can, particularly if you explain you are worried.

Try and choose a time when the baby might be asleep (difficult, I know!) and other children are not just coming home from playschool or school, so that you can talk without distractions. Sally wrote about her two crying babies, the youngest one still a handful at nine months. 'I really have felt so alone with the problems of crying. I think health visitors are very important, and I have rung mine quite a few times when I'm desperate and she will come over and talk about the problem. Mine suggested sending Adam to a childminder whilst Katie is at playgroup . . . I feel this will be a help, just so I can have some time to myself.'

Your health visitor may not realise things are not going well unless you tell her. Many mothers are clever at hiding their feelings and inability to cope, but do try and confide your feelings and your health visitor should understand and support you. She may not have had children herself, but she does see hundreds of babies every year and will have come across similar problems before, and she will be able to draw on her experience of how other parents coped with the situation.

Try and see your health visitor not just as a professional adviser, but as a friend too. My health visitor has been a tremendous source of help and encouragement. Rhona too found her health visitor helped her a great deal when she was struggling with a crying baby and breastfeeding problems. She says 'The turning point came when my very friendly health visitor called and gave me a lot of support, told me not to worry and gave me her copy of "Breast is Best"[1] and I read a bit at every feed.'

If you are unhappy about any advice your health visitor gives you, mention this to her, perhaps in the 'safety' of your own home. Mothers with young babies often feel vulnerable and sensitive to remarks. Something said casually or in good faith, can be misinterpreted.

If you find it difficult talking to your health visitor, do not give up – any relationship takes time. If you really feel that you cannot get on with her, try and see another one at the same clinic or at another clinic. You can attend any clinic for normal weighing and advice. If you would really like to change your health visitor, this should be possible. Write to the Nursing Officer (Health Visiting) at your local Health Authority (address from post office or library), and ask to be allocated another one. Your child may suffer if you turn your back on the health visiting service, as development checks for your child are very important.

Health visitors can put you in touch with local support groups, like CRY-SIS or the National Childbirth Trust[2], or simply with other mothers who are having similar problems with their babies. You can also find out about local mother and baby groups or postnatal support groups, where mothers with babies meet regularly for a chat and a coffee. If there are no facilities like this locally, ask your health visitor if she could set one up at the clinic – perhaps you could help run it.

Health visitors do tend to work office hours, from 9–5, so ask about what to do if you are really desperate in the evenings, at night or during the weekend.

Consult your midwife

Most mothers receive at least one visit at home from a community midwife shortly after the birth of the baby. The midwife is responsible for checking that you and the baby are making good progress during the first few weeks. Some mothers keep in touch with their midwife and ask them for advice.

Kim's midwife visited her shortly after she came out of hospital with her crying baby. 'My community midwife was very helpful and called in my GP to see if there was some medical reason for her lack of sleep and endless crying.'

Maternity hospital

Some parents telephone the maternity hospital where the baby was born, if they are worried about excessive crying, particularly out of office hours or if they do not want to disturb the GP or health visitor. It can be useful in the early weeks, especially if you have struck up a good relationship with the nurses – although staff on maternity wards do change frequently, so it may not be possible to track down the helpful midwife on duty when you were there.

Clinic doctor

Many clinics have a special doctor, known as a clinical medical officer, who carries out routine medical check-ups and assessments on babies and children at regular intervals. This doctor often gives vaccinations too. Take the opportunity to discuss any problems with this doctor. It may also be possible to consult the clinic doctor without an appointment at normal clinic times – ask the health visitor or clinic staff about this.

Referral to a paediatrician

Your GP may suggest that you consult a paediatrician (a child specialist) with hospital facilities about the baby's excessive crying or sleeplessness.

Your GP may want you to be reassured that the baby is healthy, or the GP may suspect a medical complication and want advice and treatment. Parents can ask their GP for a referral if they are particularly anxious. Some parents turn up at the Casualty department of a hospital hoping to see a paediatrician. Some babies are admitted this way, but some are given a brief examination, often by an inexperienced doctor, and sent home. So, it is probably best to go through the proper channels, your GP, to ensure you see the right doctor.

If your baby is admitted into hospital, you will normally be able to stay too, and if you are breastfeeding you will probably find this more convenient. Otherwise, you may be given the opportunity to stay at home for a few nights to get some rest and visit the baby during the daytimes.

The baby will be examined carefully, X-rays may be taken, urine and stool specimens will be analysed, and then the baby is observed, usually for a few days.

If you are breastfeeding, the hospital may suggest that the baby is test-weighed before and after feeds over a 24 hour period to see how much breastmilk the baby is taking. This happened when my baby and I were admitted and I was quite surprised to see how much milk he was getting; although he was feeding every two hours, one hourly in the evenings, it amounted to more than the daily requirement for a baby his age and weight. Test-weighing need not be an accurate indication either, particularly if the baby is ill or if you are tense; both may reduce the amount of milk taken.

Parents often find, as I did, that the doctors and nurses on the children's ward are very supportive and helpful. If your baby appears to be healthy, you may feel that you are taking up a valuable place in a ward of sick children, but paediatricians do take a crying baby seriously and know the pressures it puts on parents.

Special help for parents

A few doctors and psychologists have recently specialised in helping crying babies and their parents. A crying baby clinic has recently been set up by the psychologists at the Hospital for Sick Children, Great Ormond Street, London. Other similar clinics and sleep clinics have also been set up in some areas of the country. A great deal of training information can come out of these clinics which can be passed on to local doctors, health visitors and midwives to help them support parents better.

A few 'drop-in' centres, crying baby health visiting services, and 'open-door' hospital policies have been established. If you would like to find out if there is a service like any of these in your area, ask your health visitor. Unfortunately, some of these services have come to a halt because of lack of funding – or lack of commitment to the importance of these projects.

Drugs and sedatives for the baby

Your GP or paediatrician may suggest sedatives, either to calm the baby down generally so that perhaps feeding is easier, or to help the baby to sleep better. They act by surpressing the central nervous system. Sometimes they work for a short time and then become ineffective. Other times they work well. Other times they do not work at all, but produce the opposite effect desired, making the baby 'high' and overactive. Many parents find thât when sedatives do work, they are left with a 'hungover' and irritable baby the next day, but for a few hours sleep it is sometimes worth it.

The most commonly prescribed product is Phenergan. It is important to ensure the dosage is correct otherwise it is unlikely to send the baby to sleep for long if at all. Your doctor or chemist will advise you of the correct dose. A smaller dose might help colic or tummy pains. Although it is possible to buy Phenergan over the counter at your chemist, consult your doctor before giving any to your baby especially if the baby is under six months. Vallergan and Chloral are also prescribed for babies – again full doses are needed to be effective.

Make sure that the doctor has not just prescribed a medicine as an easy way out. Ensure that the problem has been fully discussed and other possibilities explored before resorting to drugs. If you decide to give the baby sedatives, it should be viewed as a short term measure to give you a break and sometimes it does achieve changing a pattern of disruptive sleep.

Sharon found that it worked for her baby. 'When Shane was about six months old, a friend suggested I try Phenergan at night for a few nights to help his sleep. Wonder of wonders, it worked and he got into the habit of taking about five or six hours uninterrupted sleep. Although he was still crying and demanding during the day, I felt much better for getting a sleep at night.'

Limitations

There are limitations to the amount of help you can reasonably expect from your medical advisers. There may seem to be nothing wrong with the baby, who may be thriving and appear perfectly healthy, although many professionals now know that some babies do cry excessively inspite of this. Many health advisers are busy and have other patients or parents to deal with, but if you feel you have a problem, do not be put off by this. Doctors and health visitors may be busy, but they do want to know and help you. There may be no suitable medicine which can be prescribed to help the baby. Lastly, your adviser's own experience with babies or crying/sleep problems may be limited. An ex-health visitor, who is now a contact for CRY-SIS, admitted that she did not have a full appreciation of the problems of a crying baby until she had one of her own!

Despite these limitations, health advisers do help parents. Nine mothers of the 59 who wrote to me specifically mentioned being helped and supported by their health visitor, GP, paediatrician or midwife.

In the *Parents Magazine* survey into crying babies, nearly half of the mothers asked for help and most of these approached their health visitors. Only a third said that the advice given actually stopped the baby crying so much, but talking about the problem helped the majority of mothers feel better. However, a worrying 42 per cent felt that the problem was not taken seriously.

Notes
1 *Breast is best*. Doctors Penny and Andrew Stanway. Pan, 1978.
2 CRY-SIS – the support group for parents of crying babies. National Childbirth Trust (NCT) offers post-natal support and support with breastfeeding. (Addresses in Appendix 1).

9

Beyond the crying

Many crying babies come to terms with life and eventually settle down. You and your baby may have got off to a bad start, but do not let this spoil your future. Your baby will get better and you will really appreciate your child. You will enjoy many experiences and have lots of happy times together. Sometimes, however, there are continued problems for parents.

Continued behaviour problems

Fourteen of the 63 babies in my survey continued to display demanding, difficult behaviour and irritability. Sometimes, this went on for several months until the child was walking and talking. Sometimes, it continued for several distressing years.

Carol wrote about her child's continued problems. 'She is still a very disruptive and temperamental child. The intervening years and months are rather jumbled in my mind. The constant crying graduated into whining and tantrums as Sophie grew older and the "happy spells" have consisted of maybe the odd day or two or a fortnight at most. Her sleeping has improved a lot (thank goodness) between two and three years old, but I find her very hard work to look after even now.'

All young children have difficult phases and bad days, when 'no' seems to be the only word they can say. But, when every day turns into a battle of wills with a child who readily bursts into tears or rage, it is very demoralising and frustrating for the parents.

Sheila found her own way of dealing with the problem. 'When my daughter was older (two and a half years onwards) I sometimes put her in the bathroom, if I felt I was getting aggressive towards her. I would give her her dummy and cuddlies. Sometimes she would go in there on her own accord when she wanted her paddy. The door was always left ajar for her to come out again when she'd finished. Sometimes we would say to her "have you finished yet?", the reply "no" and she would go back in and shut the door.'

My daughter had tantrums regularly and whined for a long time. She was always worse when alone with me. Now, I feel quite cheated out of those early years when much of the time, I longed to get away from her. If only I had known that her problems were caused by food allergies, rather than her own personality or my handling of her.

If your child continues to display difficult behaviour, consider food allergies (see sections on allergies and hyperactivity on pages 38 and 125). As the child grows older, keep the level of sugar in the diet down as much as possible. There is some evidence that large amounts of sugar can cause behavioural problems. You can decide for instance from an early age that your child will not have sweets, which are full of sugar and artificial colourings. Snacks can consist of fruit, cheese, bread or biscuits, and the occasional treat can be a piece of chocolate or some crisps. Once I cut out sweets for my children, I found they hardly ever asked for them. They also ate better at mealtimes.

Juliet thought her child's behaviour improved because she managed to give her consistently early nights and at the same time started the child on vitamin tablets, which included the B Complex vitamins.

Continued support from others and the friendship of other parents will help you through the rough times, as it did me. If you go regularly to a Mother and Toddler group, you will soon discover that other toddlers can be just as difficult or create problems in other ways. Some helpful books are also recommended in Appendix 2.

Starting your child at playschool or nursery is often a big turning point, giving you and the child a welcome break from each other and helping the child to learn more acceptable behaviour from other children and the playschool teacher. Starting school is another big help for a bright active child.

Continued sleep problems

Twenty-eight of the 63 babies whose parents contributed to this book developed long-term sleep problems. It seems to be more likely to happen to a crying baby, since poor sleeping can become a habit.

If you want to break the habit of waking at night and you are sure hunger is not the cause, try offering the baby plain boiled water which has been cooled, preferably from a feeder cup rather than a bottle, instead of a feed. Sometimes, a few nights of this will stop the baby waking up.

A practical management technique is explained in a book by two psychologists, Jo Douglas and Naomi Richman, based on their experience of running a sleep clinic at the Hospial for Sick Children, Great Ormond Street.[1] The technique to help reduce night waking includes a routine where parents are advised not to pick the child up, to leave the room quickly and wait five minutes before going to the child again.

The strategy of letting a child 'cry it out' is recommended by a few specialists for healthy babies over five or six months of age, where the baby is left to cry at night. However, there are quite a number of experts who feel it can do more harm than good.

Several parents who wrote to me resorted to this stringent method, usually when all else had failed and they were really desperate for some sleep. It did work in some cases, as one mother describes. 'Right or wrong, we decided to leave our baby to cry one night. He woke up at 1.00 a.m. and cried until 2.00 a.m., then went back to sleep (I did keep checking him). He woke up again at 4.00 a.m. and cried until 4.30 a.m. The next night and thereafter he slept through, except when teething etc.'

However, Jeannette found it did not work for her. 'Letting her "cry it out" didn't help. All that did was upset me more.'

Talk to your health visitor too about continued sleep problems. She will have lots of useful ideas. Sleeping drugs sometimes help to break a bad sleeping pattern. Consult you GP about this possibility.

Remember that allergies and sensitivities to foods and food additives can cause sleep problems in children. Hazel discovered this when she took her daughter off all cow's milk products at the age of three and a half, and her child slept for the first night in two years.

Hyperactive child

A small proportion of crying, sleepless babies turn into hyperactive children. Sally Bunday, whose third child was hyperactive, founded the Hyperactive Children's Support Group, HACSG, (see Appendix 1 for address) in 1977. Up until then, hyperactive children were normally prescribed drugs to try and calm them. However, many parents were dissatisfied with this treatment, which did not always work very well, and the parents wanted practical alternatives and more information about why their children behaved the way they did.

The parents who joined HACSG discovered that they could help themselves. Many of the children were allergy sufferers, often allergic to several different foods, and using new ideas and research from America, they discovered that a diet free from chemical food additives, particularly food colourings,[2] made tremendous improvements in their children's behaviour and sleeplessness. Some fruits and vegetables, such as orange, cucumber and apple, contain natural 'salicylates' to which these children can also be sensitive.

No-one knows for certain the incidence of hyperactivity. HACSG has received approximately 150,000 enquiries and currently receives 60–100 letters a day. Sally Bunday describes what life was like with her hyperactive son. 'He cried and screamed constantly no matter what we did. The anxiety I felt must have caused him to be more fretful. It drove me to distraction. The whole idea of food or chemical sensitivity was unknown. We were prescribed endless sedatives and antibiotics for catarrh. All contained colourings. It was over five years before we found out he was sensitive to these additives and were the underlying causes of his hyperactivity. Hours were spent rocking the child in the pram at night. Babysitters were non-existent. Despite having other children I was completely bewildered by this unhappy, unwell little chap. How he was not a battered baby is quite beyond me.'

The concept of food and chemical sensitivity accounting for disturbed behaviour in children is becoming more accepted in the medical profession. For example, the Hospital for Sick Children, Great Ormond Street, undertook a study of the diet of 76 overactive children.[3] Sixty-two improved with changes in their diet and a normal range of behaviour was achieved in 21 of these.

Many hyperactive children come from atopic (allergic) families and are more likely to be blue-eyed, blond boys. Many mothers reported them to have been hyperactive in the womb. Nearly all hyperactive children are extremely thirsty, which might be misinterpreted as hunger in babies. They frequently suffer from allergic conditions such as asthma, eczema, excessive dribbling and diarrhoea. They display behaviour disturbances and poor sleeping, and there are often problems with coordination of limbs (the baby may not crawl), clumsiness, fidgetiness, poor concentration, speech difficulty, and later, problems with reading and writing. They cannot be easily pacified and often seem to spurn affection.

Apart from dietary management, HACSG suggest that vitamin, mineral and Evening Primrose Oil supplements can help hyperactive children.[4]

Linda wrote a harrowing account of her three hyperactive children, all food allergic and close in age. All had been crying, sleepless babies with disturbed behaviour, including head banging, and frequent illness, eczema and chestiness. By the time the third child was six months old, there were serious doubts in the minds of social workers who were concerned at the mother's apparent inability to cope with her family. Linda writes 'My husband had given up his job, our marriage was breaking up, I was ill, and the children were smashing up the house. In desperation, I wrote to the Hyperactive Children's Support Group. There were tears on every page of that long letter.' A doctor confirmed that Linda's children were hyperactive and represented Linda at an assessment due to be held on her children. She continued, 'I felt as if I were on trial for our lives. Here we were, two loving parents, placed on trial before doctors, social workers and health visitors. We had done nothing wrong, only admitted there was something wrong with our children.' Fortunately, once on special diets the children's health and behaviour improved dramatically. Linda's eldest daughter at last after five years sat on her knee, kissed her and said 'I love you mummy.'

Continued relationship problems

Relationships within the family can remain unbalanced after the temporary upset. There may be long-term problems with other children or rivalry between another child and the baby. Being aware of what is happening and why will help you manage the situation better, as well as talking to other parents and your health visitor. Ruth considered what the lasting effects had been in her family and writes 'I don't think there have been many. His sister and he get on better than average on the whole, despite her asking at the time when he was going to die (a thought that often went through my mind).'

There may be continued problems with the relationship with your partner. Try and work these problems out together if possible. Many parents felt that in the long run, the crisis had brought the couple closer together.

The mother's continued problems

You may have been left with a long-term problem even though the baby has settled down. Continuing post-natal depression is an unpleasant condition which can take quite a few months or even years to get over completely. Getting help from your GP is very important, as well as continuing support from others.

Some mothers find the experience of a crying baby has knocked their confidence, which they find difficult to restore later. One mother who spoke to me said she had previously been a confident teacher holding a senior position. Her baby, who cried a lot for the first few months, depleted her confidence and she found the prospect of returning to work, which had been planned, very daunting.

There are ways to help overcome these problems, as outlined in Chapter 7, but it often takes time to feel you are a 'person' again. It might be simpler to accept that now you are more than just a 'person' – you are a mother too.

Another baby?

Ten mothers who wrote to me were afraid of having another crying baby and a few decided not to enter into another pregnancy.

However, when parents did have another baby, most of them had a different experience the next time. One mother writes 'My second son is now eighteen months and I'd looked forward to his birth with a sense of trepidation. However, he is a totally different child and is so easy and placid that when he was tiny we hardly knew he was there.'

Rhona was not put off either. She went ahead and had another baby and when she wrote to me, she was expecting her third. Susan said that having had a crying baby, she felt she could cope with anything. In fact, her second baby proved to be no trouble at all.

My advice would be to have another baby if you want one (I have always found two easier than one, in the long run). If you are unfortunate enough to have another crier, you will be more confident and will cope much better with experience behind you. If the next one is content and quiet, you will really appreciate the baby.

Can a crying baby be avoided?

Possibly not – but there are a number of ways of providing the optimum conditions for your new baby. If you plan to have a baby, take some positive steps towards improving your diet, even before you are pregnant, and certainly during pregnancy.

Foresight is an association for the promotion of pre-conceptual care (address in Appendix 1) and encourages both parents to eat plenty of unrefined foods, fresh meats, fruit and vegetables, and cut down on sugar and convenience foods. Parents are advised to come off any addictive drugs, including cigarettes, tranquilisers and alcohol. They should check for infections, particularly genito-urinary infections, like thrush, and get them treated. Parents' own food allergies should be considered and steps taken to avoid any relevant foods. Vitamin and mineral supplements are often advised.[5]

New research is being undertaken into the effects of toxic metals, like lead and cadmium, on the health of the unborn child. Vitamin and mineral deficiencies may cause problems. For example, some pregnant mothers are low on zinc, which is very important in many body functions. A simple and safe zinc 'taste' test has just been developed (see Zincatest, Appendix 1).

There is a theory that a baby can be sensitised to substances like cow's milk in the womb, although this has yet to be proved conclusively. Some mothers, who have already had one allergic baby, have been advised to cut down or omit cow's milk from their diet during the last three months of pregnancy. In some cases it does seem to have worked, although this could just be a coincidence of course. It is important to eat a balanced diet during pregnancy, so if you decide to eliminate a food, consult your GP or a hospital dietician to ensure that your diet is nutritionally adequate.

Prepare to breastfeed the baby for six months at least and try not to give any supplementary bottles of formula milk if possible. This is particularly important if your last baby was sensitive or allergic to cow's milk, or if your family suffer from allergies. Even if you had problems establishing breastfeeding with the previous baby, do not be put off. Problems can be helped with the advice of midwives, health visitors and organisations like the National Childbirth Trust and La Leche League (see Appendix 1 for addresses). It would be a good idea to get a good book on breastfeeding before you have the baby, and perhaps take it into hospital with you.

Go to antenatal classes which will prepare you physically and emotionally for childbirth, so that you can help yourself to your best ability, and possibly avoid complications, although this is not guaranteed of course. The classes run by the National Childbirth Trust teachers are particularly recommended – book early to avoid disappointment.[6] Antenatal classes will also teach you to relax. Bring up the subject of crying and sleep problems if it is not part of the course.

Plan your home, preparing yourself for the worst. Before you have the baby, organise some help in the home. Stock up the larder or freezer, and do not plan to do anything else, except look after yourself, the baby and the rest of the family. Build up a network of friends and support before the baby arrives to combat isolation and loneliness.

Consider how other societies manage their babies. Jean Liedloff wrote about a cut-off South American tribe called the Yequana in her book 'The Continuum Concept'.[7] The babies enjoy what she calls an 'in-arms' phase, continuously being held or carried, until they are old enough to voluntarily leave their mother's lap to crawl away and explore, virtually unheeded by their parents, who display great respect for the child's natural instincts. Babies sleep beside their mothers at night, suckling frequently. Jean Liedloff remarked that the babies were very placid and grew into happy and confident toddlers. During the two years she spent with these people, she hardly ever heard a baby or child cry.

Notes

1 *My child won't sleep*. Jo Douglas and Naomi Richman. Penguin, 1984.
2 The diet is called the Feingold diet and originates from Dr. Ben Feingold's book *Why your child is hyperactive*. Random House, New York, 1975.
3 *Controlled trial of oligoantigenic treatment in the hyperkinetic syndrome*. J. Egger et al. The Lancet, March 1985, 540–545.
4 HACSG has undertaken its own research into this and can provide advice for parents. Please send a letter containing details of the baby's age, weight and symptoms, plus 50p to cover postage and printing costs, to HACSG – address in Appendix 1.
5 If you would like more information on booklets and the address of a local clinic or doctor you could consult, write to Foresight (address in Appendix 1) sending a stamped addressed envelope.
6 Contact the National Childbirth Trust headquarters (address in Appendix 1) for information about local classes.
7 *The continuum concept*. Jean Liedloff. Penguin revised, 1986.

Appendix 1

Useful addresses

Please send a stamped addressed envelope when writing to a support group.

Association of Breastfeeding Mothers
131 Mayow Road, London SE26 4HZ. Tel: 01-778 4769. Breastfeeding support group.

Association for Post-Natal Illness
7 Gowan Avenue, London SW6. Post-natal depression – information and support.

Asthma Society and Friends of the Asthma Council
300 Upper Street, Islington, London N1 2XX. Tel: 01-226 2260. Information and supsport for asthma sufferers.

British Herbal Medicine Association
Lane House, Cowling, Nr. Keighley, West Yorks. BD22 0LX. Tel: 0535 34487. Information service and can refer to local qualified herbal practitioner.

British Homoeopathic Association
27a Devonshire Street, London W1N 1RJ. Tel: 01-935 2163. Publishes list of doctors and free leaflets on homoeopathy.

Coeliac Society of the UK
PO Box 220, High Wycombe, Bucks. Tel: 0494-37278. Self-help groups and information for gluten intolerance.

CRY-SIS
BM Cry-sis, London WC1N 3XX. Tel: 01-404 5011. Crying baby parents' support group. Local contacts and groups around the country.

Foresight
The Old Vicarage, Church Lane, Witley, Godalming, Surrey, GU8 5PN. Tel: Wormley 4500 (9.30 a.m. to 7.30 p.m.). Association for the promotion of pre-conceptual care.

General Council and Register of Osteopaths
1–4 Suffolk Street, London SW17 4HG. Tel: 01–839 2060. Provides list of all registered osteopaths.

Gingerbread
35 Wellington Street, London WC2E 7BN. Tel: 01-240 0953. One-parent families – support and social meetings.

Home Start
140 New Walk, Leicester LE1 7JL. Tel: Leicester 554988. Home Start schemes operate in many areas around the country – providing help in the home, support and friendship for families with young children.

Hyperactive Children's Support Group (HACSG)
59 Meadowside, Angmering, Little-hampton, West Sussex BN16 4BW. Dietary information and support for parents of hyperactive children.

Jaygee Cassettes
19 Golf Links Road, Burnham-on-Sea, Somerset, TA8 2PW. Tel: 0278 789352. Womb noise tapes (also available from Boots and W.H. Smith's).

La Leche League
BM 3424, London WC1 6XX. Tel: 01-404 5011. Breastfeeding support group.

Lullababy
Parish Lane, Kings Thorn, Hereford HR2 8AH. Tel: 0981 540288. Womb noise tapes (also available from W.H. Smith's) and Vertical Rocker, a device which suspends from ceiling and comprises a net which holds a carrycot or crib and bounces gently up and down.

Meet-A-Mum-Association (MAMA)
3 Woodside Avenue, South Nor-wood, London SE25. Tel: 01-654 3137. Support and help with isolation and loneliness.

Minder Automatic Pram Rocker
Cumbrian Specialist Developments Limited, Windermere Block, Mobet Trading Estate, Workington, Cum-bria CA14 3JD. Tel: 0900 67716. Device hangs on the pram handle and rocks pram automatically.

National Association for the Welfare of Children in Hospital
Argyle House, 29–31 Euston Road, London NW1 2SD. Tel: 01-833 2041. Advice and support for pa-rents whose children are in hospital.

National Childbirth Trust (NCT)
9 Queensborough Terrace, London W2 3TB. Tel: 01-221 3833. Antenat-al classes, post-natal support and support with breastfeeding.

National Council for One Parent Families
255 Kentish Town Road, London NW5 3LX. Tel: 01–267 1361. In-formation and support for one-parent families.

National Eczema Society
Tavistock House North, Tavistock Square, London WC1H 9SH. Tel: 01-388 4097. Information and sup-port for eczema sufferers.

National Federation of Women's Institutes
39 Eccleston Street, London SW1W 9NT. Tel: 01-730 7212. Social meet-ings for women.

National Housewives Register
245 Warwick Road, Solihull, West Midlands, B92 7AH. Tel: 021-706 1101. Social meetings and talks for housewives.

National Society for Research into Allergy
PO Box 45, Hinckley, Leicester LE10 1JY. Tel: 0455 635212. Research and self-help groups around the country for allergy sufferers.

Nippers
c/o Perinatal Research Unit, St. Mary's Hospital, Praed Street, London W2. Tel: 01-262 1280. Support group for parents of premature babies and babies in special care.

Parents Anonymous
6–9 Manor Gardens, London N7. Tel: 01-263 8919. Family problems helpline.

Twins Club Association
c/o Pooh Corner, 54 Broad Lane, Hampton, Middx. Support and social meetings for parents of twins.

Winganna Natural Fleeces
Sandy Hill Cottage, St. Ishmaela, Haverfordwest, Dyfed, Wales. Tel: 06465 403. Supplier of baby sheepskins.

Zincatest
Nature's Best Health Products Ltd., PO Box 1, 1 Lamberts Road, Tunbridge Wells, TN2 3EQ. Tel: 0892 34143. For details of zinc 'taste' test, which is both a test for deficiency and a zinc supplement.

Appendix 2

Further reading

Allergies
Allergy – Think About Food. Susan Lewis. Wisebuy, 1984. Available by post from Wisebuy Publications, PO Box 379, London NW3 1NJ. £2.95 plus 40p p & p.
Food For Thought. Maureen Minchin. Oxford University Press, 1986. £3.95.

Breastfeeding
Breast is Best. Drs. Penny and Andrew Stanway. Pan, 1978. £1.95.
Breastfeeding Matters. Maureen Minchin. Alma Publications, 1985. (Available from April 1987 in UK, Unwin paperback at £3.95).
The Breastfeeding Book. Maire Messenger. Century, 1982. £4.95.

General
The Baby Massage Book. Tina Heinl. Coventure, 1982. £5.25.
Baby Gymnastics. A. Balaskas and P. Walker. Unwin, 1982. £5.50.
Baby Relax. Peter Walker. Unwin, 1986. (Massage and Gymnastics) £5.95.
Dream Babies. Christina Hardyment, Jonathan Cape, 1983. (Historical perspective of attitudes towards childcare) £9.95.
A Woman In Your Own Right. Anne Dickson. Quartet Books, 1982. (Assertiveness and you) £3.95.

Gifted children
Helping The Child Of Exceptional Ability. Susan Leyden. Croom Helm, 1985. £8.95.

Herbal remedies
The Home Herbal. Barbara Griggs. Pan, 1982. £1.95.

Hyperactivity
The Hyperactive Child: What The Family Can Do. Belinda Barnes and Irene Colquhoun. Thorsons, 1984. £1.99.

Prematurity
Born Too Soon. M. Redshaw, M. Rivers and D. Rosenblatt. Oxford University Press, 1985. £7.50.

Post-Natal depression
Post-Natal Depression. Vivienne Welburn. Fontana, £2.50.
Towards Happy Motherhood: Understanding Post-Natal Depression. Margaret Comport. Corgi, due to be published in 1987.

Toddlers
Coping With Young Children. Jo Douglas and Naomi Richman. Penguin, 1984. £1.75.
Living With A Toddler. Brenda Crowe. Unwin, 1980. £2.50.

Sleep problems
My Child Won't Sleep. Jo Douglas and Naomi Richman. Penguin, 1984. £1.95.
Sleepless Children. Dr. David Haslam. Futura, 1984. £1.95.

Special diets
E For Additives. Maurice Hanssen with Jill Marsden. Thorsons, 1984. £2.95.
Happiness Is Junk Free Food. Janet Ash and Dulcie Roberts. Thorsons, 1986. (Milk-free, gluten-free and additive-free recipes), £2.99.
The Foresight Wholefood Cookbook. Norman and Ruth Jervis. Aurum, 1986. £5.95.
Wysoy Milk-Free Cookery. Free Wyeth nutrition booklet – enquire with your health visitor or clinic.

Appendix 3

Analysis of 63 crying babies

Letters were received from 59 mothers, some had had more than one crying baby, one father and one midwife (these two did not have crying babies). There were 63 babies in total (30 boys and 33 girls). 19 mothers reported obstetric or pregnancy complications.

Infant feeding
19 Babies were totally breastfed.
17 Were bottlefed.
14 Did not specify.
13 Were breastfed for a few weeks, then bottlefed.

Position in the family
46 First babies.
12 Second babies.
 2 Third babies.
 1 Fourth baby.
 2 Did not specify.

Age of onset of crying
46 Birth to one week.
10 One week to three weeks.
 4 Three weeks to three months.
 3 Later.

Age at end of crying
 7 Nil to three months.

26 Three to six months.
 5 Six to nine months.
25 Over nine months.

Length of time crying persisted
 9 One week to three months.
23 Three months to six months.
31 Six months and longer.

What helped the baby (reported by mother)
23 Discovery of allergies.
10 Dummy.
 9 Movement (sling, car rides, pram rides).
 7 Breastfeeding.
 3 Cassette of womb sounds.
 2 Cranial osteopathy.
 1 Drugs.

What helped mothers
20 Actual help from others (eg marvellous husbands, own mother, sister, friend, neighbour).
10 Talking to others, particularly support groups.
 6 Putting baby out of earshot, when mother felt she could not stand the crying any more.
 9 GP, health visitor, midwife or Paediatrician.
 5 Left baby to 'cry it out'.
Other mothers mentioned as helpful Toddler Groups, going for walks with the pram, going to friends' houses.

Long-term problems
Baby:
28 Long-term sleep problems.
14 Tantrums and behaviour problems.
 7 Continued allergies.
 2 Continued dummy.
Mother:
14 Depression (very serious in a few instances).
10 Fear of having another baby.

Index

ALLERGY?
THINK
ABOUT FOOD

'I am glad to be able to recommend a book which lists all additives at the back called Allergy? Think About Food.'
Katie Boyle, TV Times

'I received the copy of Allergy? Think About Food which to my mind is the best on the market of its kind. Would you kindly let me have two more copies which I want to pass on to friends.'
Mrs M. R. Oxford

'If you want to find out whether food or drink is the cause of your – your child's – allergy, Susan Lewis has written a helpful, easy-to-understand book.'
Weekend

To: **Wisebuy Publications, PO Box 379, London NW3 1NJ**

Please send me _____ copies of ALLERGY? THINK ABOUT FOOD at £2.95 per copy plus 40p p & p or £5 airmail (US $8).

I enclose cheque/PO for £ _____ payable to Wisebuy Publications

Name _____
Block letters please

Address _____

_____

_____ Post code _____

ALLERGY?
THINK
ABOUT FOOD

'One of the major problems with many additives is that they are known to cause allergies. If you do have one which you cannot trace, it would be worth investing in a paperback called Allergy? Think About Food.'
Daily Telegraph

'In her practical, very readable book she is at pains to point out that just because one food cause similar symptoms in somebody else it does not necessarily account for your own.'
Sunday Times

'. . . the book is packed with useful practical information and could be recommended to people who have just realised that their food might be affecting them . . .'
Society of Environmental Therapy

'Anyone who wants to find out if they or their children have an allergy to a food or drink would find this a useful book.'
Nursing Mirror

With the help of real life examples, Susan Lewis documents how ordinary men and women found that sometimes serious and disabling conditions could be cured 'miraculously'. Rashes, wheezing, headaches, hyperactivity, bedwetting, stomach upsets, aches and pains, and even mental illness disappeared once a food or drink was eliminated.
Order your copy overleaf